Sweeten Your Life the Xylitol Way

SECOND EDITION

Delicious recipes using nature's own low-calorie sweetener

Karen Edwards, Ph.D.

Illustrations by Raymond Hunt

Sweeten Your Life the Xylitol Way
by Karen Edwards, Ph.D.

ISBN 0-9746045-2-6

Design by Armour&Armour, Nashville, Tennessee

First Edition 2003

Second Edition 2006

5 6 7 8 9 10 11

Contents

Preface to the Second Edition

I would like to thank everyone who has purchased the first two printings of the hard-bound version and the multiple printings of the soft-bound version of this unique cookbook. When I started out to compile the recipes and self-publish the book, I was unsure as to what kind of response it would generate. The response was very gratifying, and after the second printing sold out, I realized that there was a real demand for a cookbook that utilized xylitol as the only sweetener.

Prior to the third printing, I decided to update some of the original recipes as I continued to experiment and improve my cooking methods. As I learned better and more efficient ways to make the recipes even more tasty, satisfying, and eye-appealing, I also began to develop new recipes based on some of the favorite desserts that people have desired but may have had to forego because of health concerns. I also had received some valuable feedback from people who had tried the recipes themselves or had eaten some of the desserts that I had made.

This second edition combines the updated recipes along with many new recipes and includes some new information about xylitol. The price per pound remains higher than that of refined sugar, but has moderated somewhat as the supply has increased. Other natural sweeteners have now entered the mainstream offering some of the same healthful benefits as xylitol. Erythritol, for instance, has basically zero carbohydrates and zero glycemic index with no negative digestive effects. It is only 60 to 70 percent as sweet as xylitol and costs more per pound, however. Stevia has now been accepted by the FDA as an alternative sweetener, and has no known negative side effects, must be used in small amounts because of its aftertaste and it does not provide the necessary bulk for most desserts or baked products when used by itself. Maltitol, on the other hand, has much greater gastric side effects than xylitol and has a higher glycemic index along with a “flat” taste.

I trust that you will find this version of the cookbook even more appealing than the first edition, and hope that the new recipes will stimulate even more interest in xylitol and the use of whole grains. By eliminating refined sugar and refined flour from our diet, we can gain tremendous benefits to our health.

Please feel free to contact me by e-mail at *karen@karenshealthykitchen.com* if you have questions, suggestions, or comments about the recipes, or if you wish to have more information on anything in the book. I recommend that you use a search engine to see for yourself the large amount of information now available on the internet about xylitol.

Good luck and good cooking in the future!

Karen Edwards

Foreword

The value of xylitol as a sugar substitute was demonstrated in the famous "Turku Sugar Studies" which were conducted in Finland during the early 1970's. Food suppliers were invited to come up with xylitol versions of their standard recipes. After considerable mixing, tweaking, and adjusting, a full line of xylitol replacements emerged. Among these were xylitol pastries, cookies, jams, yogurt, ice cream, candy, soft drinks, pickles, relish, mustard, and ketchup. One group of young adult volunteers was given these specially prepared foods in which xylitol replaced sugar wherever possible. Most of them considered their xylitol diet comparable or superior to a regular sugar diet. The most outstanding finding from Turku was that a xylitol diet practically eliminated the development of tooth decay. The results were so encouraging that a parallel study was begun to test xylitol in chewing gum. Used this way, xylitol produced similar dental benefits at a much lower consumption level.

For the next 20 years, research focused on using small amounts of xylitol in delivery systems targeted to protect teeth. During this time, xylitol was considered too scarce and expensive to be practical as a general purpose sugar substitute. In some countries such as Germany and Russia, xylitol continued to be used as a premium sweetener in the diabetic diet. More recently there has been a trend for an increased supply and decreased price for xylitol. This has prompted more interest in xylitol for applications beyond chewing gum and toothpaste. Consumers found that xylitol has many qualities that make it suitable for their dietary goals: good functional sweetness with reduced calories and very low Glycemic Index (reduced impact on blood sugar and insulin). There is also evidence for some prebiotic and satiety effects. Some of these beneficial properties result from the slow absorption and metabolism of xylitol. As with dietary fiber (think beans!), too much xylitol at one time can lead to intestinal gas and loose stools. Most people adapt quickly to tolerate increasing amounts of xylitol. Begin by using a small amount of xylitol, such as gum or mints, after each meal. Allow yourself two weeks to gradually build up your comfort level.

It is interesting to look back at the Turku studies and realize that the sugar consumption level was only about half of what much of the population consumes today. Even with a healthy sweet such as xylitol, moderation is the sensible approach. Have fun with the recipes, and enjoy a little sweetness. The smiles are worth it.

John Peldyak, D.M.D.
July 2003

Introduction

There must be literally thousands of cookbooks of all kinds, sizes, and types of cuisine on the market today. I have seen everything from vegan cookbooks to recipes using Coca-Cola. Why in the world then would I want to compile another cookbook with so much competition out there? The idea started with a vague feeling that somehow there was a relationship between the food I was eating and my overall health. Over a period of several years I became more aware of my body and that I had developed a host of chronic medical concerns. At first I blamed the majority of these on heredity, noting that many of my relatives had experienced similar health problems over the years and had developed even more serious conditions such as cancer and heart disease. I knew that I did not want my health to deteriorate to the point where I might also develop these diseases. Because I had begun to have less and less success in improving my health using conventional medical techniques and treatments, I began an intensive search into more natural healing methods.

As my awareness of alternative healing methods increased, I realized that I wanted a more formal education in this field than I could get through simply reading magazine articles, talking to others about their anecdotal experiences and gleaning information from an herbal company with which I had become associated. I decided to enroll in Clayton College of Natural Health in Birmingham, Alabama, because they offered a program and degrees in holistic nutrition, and I could complete the course of study at home. I had always enjoyed cooking and preparing meals that were not only healthy but were also satisfying to the taste, and I thought that combining this interest with a more thorough knowledge of nutrition would benefit not only me, but my husband as well.

As I progressed through my studies, I learned more and more details about the effects that different foods have on the body and which foods were most beneficial to our health. Foods that have undergone the least amount of refining contain more nutrients than highly refined foods, and consequently, are better able to help restore optimal health within the body. On the other hand, highly refined and processed foods, while appealing to the sensory pleasures of taste, smell, and texture, are in most cases devoid of the nutrients necessary for the body to maintain optimal health.

For several years I had been compiling a number of traditional recipes that I had modified using healthier ingredients. For instance, I used honey, molasses, and organic sugar as sweeteners, but even though these natural sweeteners were more nutritious than refined sugar, research into nutrition for my doctorate showed that they not only fed the bacteria that caused tooth decay, they also contributed to other unhealthy situations (i.e., elevated blood sugar levels, ear, bladder and yeast infections). I began to search for other alternative sweeteners to replace those in my recipes, and found two products that met my requirements: stevia and xylitol. Stevia, while much sweeter than sugar, could only be used in small quantities, and did not give adequate results because of its lack of bulk in making desserts. However, I learned that granulated xylitol could be substituted directly for sugar, and I decided to try it in recipes that I made for my family and friends. The results were so outstanding that I was able to modify almost all of my recipes so that xylitol was the only sweetener used. I discovered two exceptions to the general rule that xylitol can be substituted directly for sugar. These are that xylitol does not caramelize or brown similar to refined sugar and it also will not feed yeast, which prevents it from being used in recipes where dough needs to rise. However, xylitol can be used in most other types of baked goods and desserts.

People began to ask for my recipes, but they had never heard of xylitol and were unaware that it occurs naturally in fruits and vegetables. Some of my acquaintances were fearful that it was an artificial sweetener such as aspartame or saccharin. I had already planned to publish a cookbook for people who were wishing to make the transition from traditional recipes to a healthier cooking style. This cookbook contained all types and kinds of recipes for a wide variety of foods including desserts. I mentioned this cookbook to the lady with the company I usually ordered xylitol from, and she was so interested that she insisted that I talk to the product manager of the company. He was very interested also and encouraged me to write a cookbook with recipes using xylitol exclusively as the sweetener, because there were no cookbooks of this type on the market.

Based on the overwhelmingly positive response from my family and friends to the modified recipes and because of the encouragement of the product manager, I decided to write this cookbook. My goals are to help others become more aware of the benefits derived from using xylitol as a sweetener and to show how easy it is to use. Because most of us enjoy at least an occasional dessert, I have proven that recipes made with whole foods, including whole grain flours and other nutritious ingredients along with xylitol as the primary sweetener, can taste delicious and have an appealing texture. We can now enjoy a treat without all of the guilt normally associated with sweets and realize that healthy foods can truly taste good. In order to increase the nutritional value of these recipes, I have also eliminated refined flours, and reduced the fat content in many of the recipes by 50 percent or more.

I hope you get as much enjoyment and benefits from making these recipes as I have, and I encourage you to experiment further with your own recipes to make them healthier using xylitol along with more natural ingredients.

About Xylitol

WHAT IS IT?

Xylitol is a naturally occurring sweetener that is found in raspberries, strawberries, plums, corn, endive, and mushrooms, and it is produced by the human body during its normal metabolism of glucose at the rate of about 10 to 15 grams daily. It is a five-carbon sugar alcohol, or polyol (chemical formula: $C_5H_{12}O_5$; molecular weight: 152.15), that can be synthesized from a number of natural products such as corn cobs or the bark of birch trees. Even though commercial xylitol is synthesized, it is considered a natural substance because its chemical composition is identical to the naturally occurring substance. It is an odorless white crystalline powder with the same sweetness and bulk as sucrose (sugar), but having 40% less calories. It is metabolized in the body as a normal carbohydrate, but at a much slower rate than sucrose. Xylitol has a glycemic index of 7 as compared to that of sugar which is 64 and glucose which is 100. It has no aftertaste and also has a very pleasant cooling sensation when it dissolves in the mouth.

HISTORY

Xylitol was discovered in 1891 by Emil Fischer, a German chemist. It was used chiefly as a research chemical until World War II resulted in a shortage of sugar in some European countries such as Finland. Finnish researchers and engineers succeeded in developing an industrial method for xylitol production on a small scale to provide an alternative sweetener. However, the end of the war removed the sugar shortage, and xylitol production was not pursued again until 1975 when the Finns began large-scale production. A Swiss company, F. Hoffman La-Roche, joined with the Finnish Sugar Co. in 1976 to found Xyrofin, which later became a wholly owned subsidiary of the Finnish Sugar Co. (currently Cultor). Prior to 1970, companies located in the Soviet Union, China, Japan, Germany, Italy, and others produced xylitol mainly for domestic use as a sweetener in diabetic diets or for use in infusion therapy. The first xylitol chewing gum was produced and distributed both in Finland and the United States in 1975. Today, xylitol is not only available in bulk form, but is also found in many products such as mints, toothpastes, mouthwashes, confections, pharmaceuticals, and dietetic and diabetic foods.

MEDICAL INFORMATION

Because of xylitol's unique 5-carbon structure, many types of bacteria such as Streptococcus mutans cannot metabolize it. This is the key reason that xylitol has been found to be effective in preventing or reducing cavities and sinus infections and inhibiting the growth of bacteria that cause ear infections in children. A number of research studies conducted over more than 30 years have confirmed that using xylitol in the form of chewing gum from 3 to 5 times a day (about 4 to 12 grams a day) will reduce or prevent dental caries. In the United States, xylitol is approved as a food additive in unlimited quantities for foods with special dietary purposes. Xylitol is useful as a sweetener in foods for persons who have diabetes because of its low glycemic index and its reduced caloric value (2.4 calories per gram vs. 4.0 for sugar). This was the first medical use of xylitol. Insulin is required to get glucose into the cells, which is a problem for diabetics. Because xylitol is metabolized into glycogen that can be stored directly in the cells until it is converted into glucose for energy, no insulin is therefore required. Also, because xylitol is slowly absorbed and is a natural insulin stabilizer, the rapid rise in blood glucose levels normally associated with the ingestion of sugar is greatly reduced. Another benefit of xylitol is prevention of Candida Albicans because it inhibits yeast growth. It also increases the absorption of B vitamins and calcium, thus aiding in the prevention of the onset of osteoporosis. Studies in Finland have shown evidence that xylitol can actually reverse bone loss. Recent research by the University of Iowa has found promising evidence that xylitol may be helpful in preventing lung infections in cystic fibrosis patients, and experimentation is continuing.

SAFETY

Xylitol is considered safe for human consumption and is an approved food additive. The Federation of American Societies for Experimental Biology confirmed this in a study in 1986 prepared at the request of the U.S. Food and Drug Administration, which approved its use as a sweetener in 1963. The Joint Expert Committee on Food Additives not only verified that xylitol was safe for humans, but also discounted adverse findings in a 1970 animal study by stating that a review of the results were found not to be relevant to humans. This committee, which is an advisory body to the World Health Organization and the United Nations, allocated an Acceptable Daily Intake of "not specified" which is the safest category that a food additive can be given. In addition, the European Union has accepted xylitol as acceptable for dietary use. According to the American Society for the Prevention of Cruelty to Animals Poison Control Center, xylitol, when ingested by dogs, can pose a considerable risk of toxicosis to them due to an increase of blood insulin levels that results in significantly diminished blood glucose levels.

DISADVANTAGES

There are few disadvantages to xylitol. It is more expensive than sugar and is not as easily found in grocery stores. If xylitol has never been used before, ingesting a large amount at one time may result in temporary gastrointestinal discomfort. However, this problem disappears quickly because the body not only produces it during normal metabolism but also

continued on next page

continued from previous page

produces the enzymes necessary to break it down. Therefore, adaptation to the use of xylitol is very rapid. Regular use reduces this small side effect, and most people can accept about 100 grams daily if individual servings are limited to 20 to 30 grams each when xylitol is first incorporated into the diet.

THE FUTURE

There are a number of research programs now underway in the USA and other countries to make xylitol from less costly raw materials and to reduce the production cost by utilizing new and more efficient methods. For instance, the Agricultural Research Service is developing a way to synthesize xylitol using a biotechnological approach involving the leftover corn fiber from ethanol production. This method should require less energy than the processes now being used. The U.S. Army is now preparing to include xylitol sweetened chewing gum in the Soldiers' Meals Ready to Eat (MREs) to alleviate the increase in tooth decay noted in soldiers returning from Iraq. The American Dental Association through an article in their Journal has expressed interest in the use of xylitol-containing products to help control dental caries. As the popularity of using xylitol increases and the resulting sales volume increases, the cost will certainly decrease in the future.

For more information concerning xylitol, the following references are listed for your convenience:

1. "Xylitol, Sweeten Your Smile", a booklet by John Peldyak, DMD, 1996, now out of print but can be found on the Internet through used bookstores or downloaded from www.xylitol.org.
2. http://www.laleva.cc/food/xylitol.html; article, "Xylitol: Our Sweet Salvation?" by Sherrill Sellman, from The SPECTRUM Vol.4 No.8; February 2003, p. 23.
3. www.caloriecontrol.org/xylitol.html
4. www.principalhealthnews.com, search for "xylitol"
5. www.xylitolinfo.com
6. www.tifac.org.in/news/view6.htm
7. www.nasal-xylitol.com/xylitol.html
8. www.pharmj.com/Editorial/20001014/clinical/xylitol_543.html
9. http://xylitol.org/dr_greene.asp
10. http://en.wikipedia.org/wiki/Xylitol
11. http://www.nutrition.org/cgi/content/full/128/10/1811
12. http://www.vrp.com/thearticles.asp?article=717

Helpful Hints for Using These Recipes

In today's hectic, fast-paced world, it appears that an increasing number of people are searching for quick and easy recipes with a minimum number of ingredients. In compiling these recipes, I have focused on using whole foods and the freshest ingredients. I have found that employing this combination of top-quality ingredients produces delicious results that are far more satisfying than those recipes that are made from mixes found in grocery stores and foods prepared by even the best restaurants. These hints are offered to help you obtain optimal flavor and health benefits from the recipes in this cookbook.

SELECTING FRUIT: When preparing a recipe requiring fruit, select fruit at its peak of ripeness, because fruit that has ripened has a fuller, richer, and sweeter flavor than fruit that has not fully ripened or is overripe. Also it should be noted that overripe or under ripe fruit, or fruit that has had a long storage period, loses essential nutrients such as vitamins and enzymes.

ORGANIC INGREDIENTS: Buy and use organic ingredients whenever possible. This is becoming more important every day in order to avoid toxins such as herbicides, pesticides, by products of the petrochemical industries, emulsifiers, antibiotics, and growth hormones. In addition, organic produce is grown with natural fertilizers that contain all of the necessary minerals needed to grow healthy plants, whereas artificial fertilizers contain only a small portion of these vital minerals. Organic fruits should be washed under running water and scrubbed with a vegetable brush before using. If organic fruits are not used, be sure to scrub them with a vegetable brush after spraying with a produce cleanser and then rinse or soak thoroughly.

PIE SHELLS: Pre-baking a pie shell is sometimes necessary in order to avoid a soggy crust. To pre-bake the bottom crust, fit the pastry into the pie plate, and refrigerate for at least 30 minutes before baking to keep the decorative edging intact when it is placed into the pre-heated oven. Remove from the refrigerator, line the pastry with parchment paper covering the edge of the crust, and fill with any type of dried beans, which can be reused many times. Bake at 425° for 15 minutes, and remove the pie shell from the oven. Remove the beans and parchment paper. Using a fork, prick completely through the pastry all over the bottom and sides to prevent bubbles from forming.

continued on next page

continued from previous page

If a filling containing a large amount of liquid such as a custard-type filling is to be added, then prick only halfway through the pastry with the fork. Return the pie shell to the oven, and bake for an additional 5 minutes prior to adding the filling.

PAN SIZE: The size of the pans used in baking cakes is critical. If the pan used is smaller than required, the batter may rise excessively and spill over the edge of the pan, or the cake may sink in the middle as it cools. Another result of using too small a pan is a coarse-textured cake. If the pan used is larger than required, the cake will look flat because it will not be able to rise sufficiently. Make sure that baking pans are one-half to two-thirds full of batter.

ICE CREAM: The ice cream recipes in this book make just the right amount to use in a small, automatic ice cream maker. To prevent ice crystals from forming on ice cream when storing it in the freezer, wrap the container in heavy aluminum foil each time it is returned to the freezer.

USING MELTED CHOCOLATE: To drizzle chocolate over cakes or cookies, melt the chocolate in a microwave oven or in a double boiler on the range top. Then spoon the melted chocolate into a corner of a small, plastic resealable bag, and cut off a tiny edge of the corner. Now it is ready to use like a pastry bag.

POWDERED XYLITOL: Powdered xylitol is commercially available and can be substituted for powdered sugar on a one-to-one basis. It can also be made from granulated xylitol using a Vita-Mix or similar machine.

WATER BATH: A water bath ensures more even baking than the normal dry heat of an oven, and it is an excellent method for preventing or greatly reducing the risk of cracking the top surface of a cheesecake. This method also results in a cheesecake with a moist and creamy texture and eliminates the need for adding flour or another starch to the recipe. Place the cheesecake in a springform pan on a large sheet of heavy-duty aluminum foil, bringing the edges of the foil up the sides to the top of the pan. This will prevent any water from seeping into the cheesecake while it is baking. Place the springform pan in the center of a large roasting pan and pour in hot water to a depth of 1½". Then bake as directed by the recipe. If you prefer to not use a water bath, bake at 300 degrees for one hour, remove from oven, and allow to sit at room temperature for one hour before refrigerating.

SELECTING BAKING CHOCOLATE: I have found it to be very important to use a high quality unsweetened chocolate in these recipes. Some of the unsweetened bar chocolate on the market today seems to have a bitter or overly strong taste, even when combined with other ingredients. In developing these recipes, I used Ghiradelli unsweetened baking chocolate.

WHOLE GRAIN FLOURS: Gluten is the component of flour that makes dough elastic, helps the baked goods rise, and prevents excessive crumbling. Many whole grain flours are proportionally lower in gluten and are also proportionally heavier than all-purpose refined flour. In order to compensate for these differences, I have modified the method that I use to prepare cakes. I separate the egg yolks from the egg whites and beat the xylitol into the whites before adding them to the other ingredients. This process helps to ensure that the texture and volume of the goods will be as close as possible to those made with all-purpose flour. I have found that using a Whisper Mill to grind the whole grain groats provides me with fresh, high-quality flour that results in improved flavor of the baked goods.

GENERAL BAKING TIP: To make cleanup easier when using a non-stick spray with muffin pans, place empty muffin cup liners on a piece of wax paper or paper towel and coat with non-stick spray *before* placing them in the muffin pan and filling with batter.

Kitchen Measures and Substitutions

Liquid Measurements

¼ cup	=	2 fluid ounces
½ cup	=	4 fluid ounces
1 cup	=	8 fluid ounces
2 cups	=	16 fluid ounces
4 cups	=	32 fluid ounces
2 cups	=	1 pint
2 pints	=	1 quart
4 cups	=	1 quart

Dry Measurements

3 teaspoons	=	1 tablespoon
2 tablespoons	=	⅛ cup
4 tablespoons	=	¼ cup
5⅓ tablespoons	=	⅓ cup
8 tablespoons	=	½ cup
16 tablespoons	=	1 cup

Be sure to measure accurately. Measure dry ingredients by lightly spooning ingredient into dry measuring cup. Use flat edge of knife to level off the top after each measure. Use measuring spoons for quantities less than ¼ cup. Dip measuring spoon into ingredient to be measured, and use knife to level off the top.

Measure liquid ingredients in a glass measuring cup. Place the cup on a solid surface at eye level. Fill cup to desired mark.

Substitutions

2 tablespoons flour for thickening	= 1 tablespoon arrowroot powder
1 teaspoon baking powder	= ¼ teaspoon baking soda +½ teaspoon cream of tartar
1 cup sour cream	= 1 cup plain whole milk yogurt
1 ounce unsweetened baking chocolate	= 3 tablespoons unsweetened cocoa powder + 1 tablespoon unsalted butter
4 ounces semi-sweet chocolate bar	= 2 ounces unsweetened chocolate bar + ⅓ cup xylitol
6 ounces (1 cup) semi-sweet chocolate chips, melted	= 6 tablespoons unsweetened cocoa powder + 7 tablespoons xylitol + 4 tablespoons unsalted butter
4 ounce bar of sweet cooking chocolate	= 4 tablespoons unsweetened cocoa powder + 5 tablespoons xylitol + 3 tablespoons unsalted butter

Cakes

Angel Food Cake

1 cup plus 2 tablespoons spelt flour
  or whole wheat pastry flour
1½ cups xylitol, divided
1½ cups egg whites
1¼ teaspoons cream of tartar
¼ teaspoon salt
1 teaspoon almond extract

Place egg whites in large mixing bowl and allow to sit at room temperature for approximately 30 minutes before preparing recipe. In a medium bowl, combine flour and ½ cup xylitol. With mixer at medium speed, beat egg whites until frothy (approx. 1 minute). Add cream of tartar, salt, and almond extract. Increase speed of mixer to high and continue beating several more minutes or until whites are almost stiff, but not dry. Decrease the mixer speed to low, and gradually beat in the remaining 1 cup xylitol. Remove bowl from mixer. Spoon flour and xylitol mixture, one-fourth at a time, over the egg whites. Fold in gently with a spatula, just until blended so they are thoroughly incorporated but don't deflate the egg whites.

Pour batter into *ungreased* 10" tube pan. Use knife to cut through batter to remove large air bubbles. Gently smooth top of batter with spoon. Bake at 375° for 30-35 minutes or until light golden brown and toothpick inserted halfway between center opening and outer edge of pan comes out clean. When cake is done, remove from oven and *immediately* invert cake onto funnel or bottle and allow to cool completely before turning it right side up again. Remove from pan. Slice with a serrated knife. **Yield: 16 servings**

Notes: This recipe is more easily prepared if you use a stand mixer. Be sure to check the diameter of the bottle top for proper fit in the center opening of the tube pan before bak-

continued on next page

Angel Food Cake

continued from previous page

ing the cake. The first time I baked this cake, I hadn't checked this measurement beforehand, and had already removed the cake from the oven before I realized the bottle I had planned to use didn't fit. The extra minute or so it took to find the right size bottle allowed the cake to deflate somewhat. Baking the cake in a non-stick tube pan with a removable bottom allows the cake to be easily removed from the pan.

This cake is very light, moist and delicious, and you would never guess that it was prepared using whole grain flour. Lemon, orange or vanilla extract may be substituted in place of almond extract, if another flavor is desired. Chocolate sauce, xylitol-sweetened berries, or peaches drizzled over the top of the cake slices, and topped with whipped cream will make it even more delicious!

Per Serving: **Calories:** 77.6 **Carbs:** 21.3g **Fiber:** 0.8g
Fat: 0.3g **Sodium:** 74.3mg **Net Carbs:** 4.7g

Chocolate Angel Food Cake

Prepare as directed for Angel Food Cake, except for the following changes:

1. Use ¾ cup plus 2 tablespoons spelt flour or whole wheat pastry flour
2. Add 1/3 cup unsweetened cocoa powder, sifted, to the flour and xylitol mixture
3. Use 1½ teaspoons vanilla extract instead of the almond extract
4. Bake for 25-30 minutes or until toothpick comes out clean

Per Serving: **Calories:** 76.8 **Carbs:** 21.2g **Fiber:** 1.3g
Fat: 0.4g **Sodium:** 74.7mg **Net Carbs:** 4.2g

Applesauce Spice Cake

2 cups whole wheat pastry flour
2 teaspoons baking soda
½ teaspoon salt
1½ teaspoons cinnamon
½ teaspoon cloves
½ teaspoon nutmeg
½ teaspoon allspice
4 tablespoons unsalted butter, melted
1½ cups unsweetened applesauce
¼ cup reduced-fat sour cream
2 eggs, separated
¾ cup plus 2 tablespoons xylitol
1 cup finely chopped apples
½ cup raisins (rehydrated and chopped)

Combine flour, baking soda, salt, cinnamon, cloves, nutmeg, and allspice in a medium bowl and set aside. In another bowl, mix together melted butter, applesauce, sour cream, and egg yolks. In a large bowl, beat egg whites with mixer until soft peaks form; gradually add xylitol and beat until peaks are stiff but not dry. Using a spatula, gradually fold dry ingredients into beaten egg whites alternately with liquid ingredients, and stir just until batter is smooth. Fold in apples and raisins. Transfer the batter to a 9" x 13" baking pan that has been buttered, lined with parchment paper, and buttered again. Bake at 350° for 25 minutes or until toothpick inserted in center comes out clean. **Yield: 24 servings**

Per Serving: **Calories:** 88.6 **Carbs:** 17g **Fiber:** 1.2g
Fat: 2.9g **Sodium:** 162mg **Net Carbs:** 9.7g

Banana Cake

2 cups whole wheat pastry flour
2 teaspoons baking soda
½ teaspoon salt
4 tablespoons unsalted butter, melted
1⅓ cups pureed ripe bananas
½ cup reduced-fat sour cream
1 teaspoon vanilla extract
3 eggs, separated
1½ cups xylitol

Combine flour, baking soda, and salt in medium bowl and set aside. In another bowl, mix together melted butter, pureed bananas, sour cream, vanilla extract, and egg yolks. In a large bowl, beat egg whites with mixer until soft peaks form; gradually add xylitol and beat until peaks are stiff but not dry. Using a spatula, gradually fold dry ingredients into beaten egg whites alternately with banana mixture, and stir just until batter is smooth. Transfer batter to a 9" x 13" baking pan that has been buttered, lined with parchment paper, and buttered again. Bake at 350° for 25-30 minutes or until toothpick inserted in center comes out clean. **Yield: 24 servings**

Note: This cake is also delicious with Lemon Cream Cheese Frosting, page 93.

Per Serving: **Calories:** 88.4 **Carbs:** 16.7g **Fiber:** 0.8g
Fat: 3.4g **Sodium:** 166mg **Net Carbs:** 5.4g

Blueberry Snack Cake

Cake:
1 cup whole wheat pastry flour
⅓ cup xylitol
2 teaspoons baking powder
½ teaspoon baking soda
½ teaspoon salt
1 egg
⅓ cup reduced-fat sour cream
1½ tablespoons extra virgin olive oil
4 tablespoons unsweetened applesauce
2 teaspoons freshly squeezed lemon juice
1 cup blueberries

Topping:
⅓ cup xylitol
¼ cup whole wheat pastry flour
¼ teaspoon cinnamon
⅓ cup finely chopped almonds
1 tablespoon unsalted butter

To prepare cake batter: Combine flour, xylitol, baking powder, baking soda, and salt in a medium bowl and set aside. In another bowl, mix together egg, sour cream, oil, applesauce, and lemon juice. Add liquid ingredients all at once to flour mixture, and stir just until dry ingredients are moistened. Pour batter into a buttered 8" square pan; sprinkle with blueberries.

To prepare topping: Combine xylitol, flour, cinnamon, and almonds. Cut in butter until mixture is crumbly; sprinkle topping over blueberries. Bake at 325° for 35 minutes or until toothpick inserted in center comes out clean. Cover with foil, if necessary, during last part of baking to avoid over browning. **Yield: 16 servings**

Per Serving: **Calories:** 92.5 **Carbs:** 15.1g **Fiber:** 1.2g
Fat: 4.2g **Sodium:** 165.6mg **Net Carbs:** 6.9g

Boston Cream Pie

¾ cup plus 2 tablespoons whole wheat pastry flour
1 teaspoon baking soda
¼ teaspoon salt
3 tablespoons unsalted butter, melted
1 teaspoon vanilla extract
½ cup buttermilk
3 tablespoons reduced-fat sour cream
2 eggs, separated
⅔ cup xylitol
Vanilla Cream Custard Filling, p. 95
Chocolate Ganache, p. 88

Combine flour, baking soda, and salt in a medium bowl and set aside. In another bowl, mix together melted butter, vanilla extract, buttermilk, sour cream, and egg yolks and set aside. In a large bowl, beat egg whites with mixer until soft peaks form; gradually add xylitol and beat until peaks are stiff but not dry. Using a spatula, fold dry ingredients into beaten egg whites alternately with liquid ingredients, stirring just until batter is smooth. Pour batter into 9" cake pan that has been buttered, lined with parchment paper and buttered again. Bake at 325° for 25-30 minutes, or until a toothpick inserted in center comes out clean. Cool in pan 5 minutes, then turn out onto cake rack and cool completely. Slice cake in half horizontally to make 2 layers. Spread one layer with Vanilla Cream Custard Filling, and top with remaining cake layer. Spread Chocolate Ganache over top of cake. Refrigerate until ready to serve. **Yield: 12 servings**

Per Serving: **Calories:** 298 **Carbs:** 41.9g **Fiber:** 1.9g
Fat: 17.7g **Sodium:** 261.6mg **Net Carbs:** 10.9g

Carrot Cake

2 cups whole wheat pastry flour
2 teaspoons baking soda
½ teaspoon salt
2 teaspoons cinnamon
½ teaspoon nutmeg
⅛ teaspoon cloves
3 tablespoons unsalted butter, melted
3 tablespoons extra virgin olive oil
½ cup unsweetened applesauce
¾ cup reduced-fat sour cream
1½ teaspoons vanilla extract
4 eggs, separated
1¾ cup plus 2 tablespoons xylitol
2 cups finely grated carrots
⅔ cup chopped walnuts
⅓ cup raisins (rehydrated and chopped)

Combine flour, baking soda, salt, cinnamon, nutmeg, and cloves in a medium bowl and set aside. In another bowl, mix together melted butter, olive oil, applesauce, sour cream, vanilla extract, and egg yolks and set aside. In a large bowl, beat egg whites with mixer until soft peaks form; gradually add xylitol and beat until peaks are stiff but not dry. Using a spatula, fold dry ingredients into beaten egg whites alternately with liquid ingredients, stirring just until batter is smooth. Fold in carrots, and repeat for walnuts and raisins. Transfer the batter to a 9" x 13" baking pan that has been buttered, lined with parchment paper, and buttered again. Bake at 350° for 30-35 minutes or until a toothpick inserted in center comes out clean. **Yield: 24 servings**

Note: Delicious with Lemon Cream Cheese Frosting, page 91.

Per Serving: **Calories:** 147.1 **Carbs:** 23.1g **Fiber:** 1.5g
Fat: 7.3g **Sodium:** 177.3mg **Net Carbs:** 8.6g

Chocolate Cake Squares

2 cups whole wheat pastry flour
¼ cup unsweetened cocoa powder, sifted
2 teaspoons baking soda
½ teaspoon salt
4 tablespoons unsalted butter, melted
½ cup water
6 tablespoons prune puree, p. 104
¼ cup unsweetened applesauce
¾ cup reduced-fat sour cream
1 teaspoon vanilla extract
2 eggs, separated
1¾ cups xylitol

Combine flour, cocoa powder, baking soda, and salt in a medium bowl and set aside. In another bowl, mix together melted butter, water, prune puree, applesauce, sour cream, vanilla extract, and egg yolks. In a large bowl, beat egg whites with mixer until soft peaks form; gradually add xylitol and beat until peaks are stiff but not dry. Using a spatula, gradually fold dry ingredients into beaten egg whites alternately with liquid ingredients, and stir just until batter is smooth. Transfer the batter to a 9" x 13" baking pan that has been buttered, lined with parchment paper, and buttered again. Bake at 350° for 25 minutes or until toothpick inserted in center comes out clean. **Yield: 24 servings**

Note: Suggested cream cheese frostings that go well with this cake are: Crème de Menthe, Mocha, Peanut Butter, or Vanilla, pages 91–94.

Per Serving: **Calories:** 99.3 **Carbs:** 19.9g **Fiber:** 1.1g
Fat: 3.6g **Sodium:** 165.1mg **Net Carbs:** 6.5g

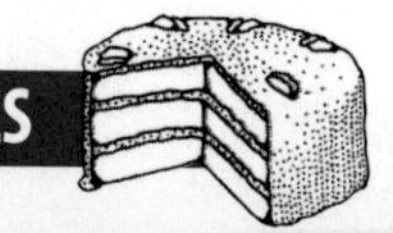

Chocolate Sour Cream Pound Cake

2½ cups plus 1 tablespoon whole wheat pastry flour
2 teaspoons baking soda
¾ teaspoon salt
6 tablespoons prune puree, p. 104
4 tablespoons unsweetened applesauce
1 cup reduced-fat sour cream
1 tablespoon vanilla extract
5 eggs, separated
½ cup unsalted butter
3 ounces unsweetened chocolate bar
2½ cups xylitol

Combine flour, baking soda, and salt in a medium bowl and set aside. In another bowl, mix together prune puree, applesauce, sour cream, vanilla extract, and egg yolks. Melt butter and chocolate together, stir well, and combine with egg mixture. In a large bowl, beat egg whites with mixer until soft peaks form; gradually add xylitol and beat until peaks are stiff but not dry. Using a spatula, gradually fold dry ingredients into beaten egg whites alternately with liquid ingredients, and stir just until batter is smooth. Pour batter into a buttered tube pan and bake at 325° for 55-60 minutes or until toothpick inserted in center comes out clean. **Yield: 20 servings**

Per Serving: **Calories:** 201.3 **Carbs:** 33.1g **Fiber:** 1.9g
Fat: 10.1g **Sodium:** 240.4mg **Net Carbs:** 10.2g

Fresh Apple Coffee Cake

Batter:
2 cups finely chopped apples
1 cup xylitol
2 tablespoons extra virgin olive oil
1 tablespoon unsweetened applesauce
1 egg, beaten
1 teaspoon vanilla extract
1½ cups spelt flour or whole wheat pastry flour
2½ teaspoons baking powder
1 teaspoon baking soda
¼ teaspoon salt
1 teaspoon cinnamon
⅛ teaspoon nutmeg
Dash of cloves

Topping:
1½ tablespoons xylitol
¼ teaspoon cinnamon
½ cup chopped pecans

Placed chopped apples and xylitol in mixing bowl; stir well, and allow mixture to sit for 30 minutes while preparing pan and remaining ingredients. Butter and flour a 9" square baking pan. In a small bowl, combine olive oil, applesauce, egg, and vanilla extract. In a separate bowl, combine flour, baking powder, baking soda, salt, cinnamon, nutmeg, and cloves. After apples and xylitol have been allowed to sit for the recommended time, stir in the egg mixture first and then stir in dry ingredients. Pour batter into prepared pan. Combine topping ingredients, and spoon evenly over batter. Bake in a 350° oven for 25-30 minutes, or until a toothpick inserted in center comes out clean. **Yield: 16 servings**

Per Serving: **Calories:** 111.4 **Carbs:** 21g **Fiber:** 1.6g
Fat: 4.6g **Sodium:** 176.4mg **Net Carbs:** 7.9g

German Chocolate Cake

Chocolate Mixture:
3 tablespoons unsweetened cocoa powder, sifted
⅓ cup xylitol
1⅔ tablespoons unsalted butter
2 teaspoons prune puree, p. 104
½ cup water

Cake:
2 ¼ cups whole wheat pastry flour
2 teaspoons baking soda
½ teaspoon salt
½ cup unsalted butter, melted
¼ cup prune puree, p. 104
¾ cup reduced-fat sour cream
1 teaspoon vanilla extract
4 eggs, separated
1¾ cups plus 3 tablespoons xylitol

To prepare chocolate mixture: In a saucepan, combine above ingredients. Cook over low heat, stirring constantly until mixture is smooth. Remove from heat and allow to cool.

To prepare cake batter: Combine flour, baking soda, and salt in a medium bowl and set aside. In another bowl, mix together melted butter, prune puree, sour cream, vanilla extract, and egg yolks; combine with cooled chocolate mixture. In a large bowl, beat egg whites with mixer until soft peaks form; gradually add xylitol and beat until peaks are stiff but not dry. Using a spatula, gradually fold dry ingredients into beaten egg whites, alternately with liquid ingredients, and stir just until batter is smooth. Transfer batter to a 9" x 13" pan that has been buttered, lined with parchment paper, and buttered again. Bake at 350° for 35-40 minutes or until toothpick inserted in center comes out clean. **Yield: 24 servings**

Note: The traditional frosting for this cake is Coconut-Pecan Frosting, page 90.

Per Serving: **Calories:** 139.5 **Carbs:** 23.8g **Fiber:** 1.1g
Fat: 6.8g **Sodium:** 171.1mg **Net Carbs:** 6.8g

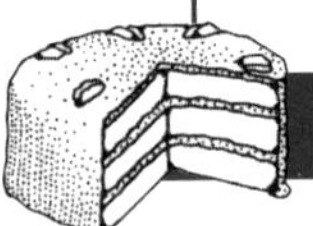

Heavenly Spice Cake

2 cups whole wheat pastry flour
1 teaspoon cinnamon
1 teaspoon allspice
1 teaspoon nutmeg
2 teaspoons baking soda
½ teaspoon salt
4 tablespoons unsalted butter, melted
3 tablespoons prune puree, p.104
¼ cup unsweetened applesauce
1 cup reduced-fat sour cream
2 eggs, separated
1½ cups xylitol
⅔ cup finely chopped prunes (cooked and drained)

Frosting:

2 tablespoons unsalted butter
½ cup reduced-fat sour cream
1 egg, lightly beaten
⅔ cup xylitol
½ cup finely chopped prunes (cooked and drained)
½ cup chopped pecans

Combine first six ingredients in medium bowl; set aside. In another bowl, mix melted butter, prune puree, applesauce, sour cream, and egg yolks. In large bowl, beat egg whites with mixer until soft peaks form; gradually add xylitol and beat until peaks are stiff but not dry. Using spatula, gradually fold dry ingredients into egg whites alternately with liquid ingredients; stir just until batter is smooth. Fold in chopped prunes. Transfer to 9" x 13" baking pan that has been buttered, lined with parchment paper, and buttered again. Bake at 350° for 25-30 minutes or until toothpick inserted in center comes out clean.

To prepare frosting: In saucepan, combine butter, sour cream, egg, and xylitol. Cook over medium low heat, stirring constantly, until slightly thickened. Stir in prunes and pecans. Allow to cool completely before spreading over cooled cake. Refrigerate frosted cake until ready to serve. **Yield: 24 servings**

Per Serving: **Calories:** 160 **Carbs:** 27.1g **Fiber:** 1.1g
Fat: 7.5g **Sodium:** 173.4mg **Net Carbs:** 10.8g

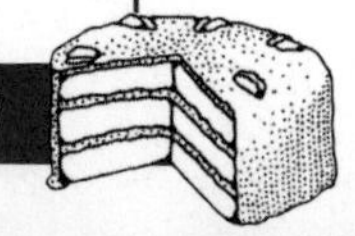

Italian Cream Cake

2 cups whole wheat pastry flour
2 teaspoons baking soda
½ teaspoon salt
3 tablespoons unsalted butter, melted
3 tablespoons extra virgin olive oil
½ cup unsweetened applesauce
½ cup buttermilk
¾ cup reduced-fat sour cream
2 teaspoons vanilla extract
5 eggs, separated
1¾ cups xylitol
1½ cups unsweetened coconut, shredded
1 cup finely chopped pecans

Combine flour, baking soda, and salt in a medium bowl and set aside. In another bowl, mix together melted butter, olive oil, applesauce, buttermilk, sour cream, vanilla extract, and egg yolks. In a large bowl, beat egg whites with mixer until soft peaks form; gradually add xylitol and beat until peaks are stiff but not dry. Using a spatula, gradually fold dry ingredients into beaten egg whites alternately with liquid ingredients, and stir just until batter is smooth. Fold in coconut and pecans. Transfer batter to a 9" x 13" baking pan that has been buttered, lined with parchment paper, and buttered again. Bake at 350° for 30-35 minutes, or until toothpick inserted in center comes out clean. **Yield: 24 servings**

Note: A suggested frosting that complements this cake well is Vanilla Cream Cheese Frosting, page 94.

Per Serving: **Calories:** 184.7 **Carbs:** 21.3g **Fiber:** 2.1g
Fats: 12g **Sodium:** 179.9mg **Net Carbs:** 7g

Kahlua Cake

1 tablespoon instant coffee powder
¾ cup boiling water
1 cup pitted dates, finely chopped
½ cup Kahlua (coffee liqueur)
2½ cups plus 2 tablespoons whole wheat pastry flour
1½ teaspoons lecithin granules
2 teaspoons baking soda
¾ teaspoon salt
¼ teaspoon cinnamon
4 tablespoons unsalted butter, melted
½ cup unsweetened applesauce
¾ cup reduced-fat sour cream
1 teaspoon vanilla extract
2 teaspoons maple flavoring
3 eggs, separated
1½ cups xylitol

In a medium bowl, dissolve coffee powder in boiling water. Stir in dates and Kahlua and allow to cool. Combine flour, lecithin granules, baking soda, salt, and cinnamon in a separate bowl and set aside. In another bowl, mix together melted butter, applesauce, sour cream, vanilla extract, maple flavoring, and egg yolks; combine with cooled Kahlua mixture. In a large bowl, beat egg whites with mixer until soft peaks form; gradually add xylitol and beat until peaks are stiff but not dry. Using a spatula, gradually fold dry ingredients into beaten egg whites alternately with liquid ingredients, and stir just until batter is smooth. Transfer the batter to a 9" x 13" baking pan that has been buttered, lined with parchment paper, and buttered again. Bake at 350° for 30-35 minutes or until toothpick inserted in center comes out clean. **Yield: 24 servings**

Per Serving: **Calories:** 144.7 **Carbs:** 27.5g **Fiber:** 1.7g
Fat: 3.9g **Sodium:** 192.7mg **Net Carbs:** 15.4g

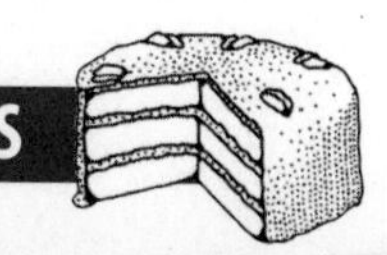

Maple Butter Pecan Cake

1½ tablespoons unsalted butter
1 cup finely chopped pecans
2 cups whole wheat pastry flour
2 teaspoons baking soda
½ teaspoon salt
¾ teaspoon nutmeg
3 tablespoons unsalted butter, melted
3 tablespoons extra virgin olive oil
½ cup unsweetened applesauce
¾ cup buttermilk
⅓ cup reduced-fat sour cream
2 teaspoons maple flavoring
4 eggs, separated
1 ⅔ cup xylitol

Melt 1½ tablespoons butter in a small baking dish. Stir in pecans and bake at 350° for 10 minutes. Allow to cool while preparing cake batter.

Combine flour, baking soda, salt, and nutmeg in a medium bowl and set aside. In another bowl, mix together melted butter, olive oil, applesauce, buttermilk, sour cream, maple flavoring, and egg yolks. In a large bowl, beat egg whites with mixer until soft peaks form; gradually add xylitol and beat until peaks are stiff but not dry. Using a spatula, gradually fold dry ingredients into beaten egg whites alternately with liquid ingredients, and stir just until batter is smooth. Fold in 1 cup toasted pecans. Transfer the batter to a 9" x 13" baking pan that has been buttered, lined with parchment paper, and buttered again. Bake at 350° for 25-30 minutes or until toothpick inserted in center comes out clean. **Yield: 24 servings**

Note: Maple Butter Pecan Frosting, page 92, is an excellent choice to top this cake.

Per Serving: **Calories:** 146 **Carbs:** 19.4g **Fiber:** 1.3g
Fat: 8.7g **Sodium:** 174.4mg **Net Carbs:** 6.4g

Overnight Coffee Cake

Cake:
4 tablespoons unsalted butter
1 cup xylitol
6 tablespoons unsweetened applesauce
2 eggs
1 cup reduced-fat sour cream
2 cups whole wheat pastry flour
1 ½ tablespoons lecithin granules
1 teaspoon baking powder
1 teaspoon baking soda
½ teaspoon salt
1 teaspoon nutmeg

Topping:
⅔ cup xylitol
½ cup finely chopped pecans
1 teaspoon cinnamon

To prepare cake batter: Cream butter and xylitol, gradually adding applesauce during creaming process. Beat in eggs. Add sour cream and mix well. Combine flour, lecithin, baking powder, baking soda, salt, and nutmeg; gradually add to cake batter and mix well. Pour batter into a buttered and floured 9" x 13" pan.

To prepare topping: Combine xylitol, pecans, and cinnamon. Sprinkle evenly over batter. Cover cake and refrigerate at least 8 hours or overnight. Uncover and bake at 350° for 25-30 minutes or until toothpick inserted in center comes out clean. **Yield: 24 servings.**

Note: This sweet, delicately-flavored coffee cake has a very light and tender texture and is better when served warm.

Per Serving: **Calories:** 117 **Carbs:** 19.1g **Fiber:** 1.1g
Fat: 5.7g **Sodium:** 129.2mg **Net Carbs:** 6.3g

Pineapple Upside-Down Cake

Topping:
3 tablespoons unsalted butter
15¼ ounce can sliced pineapple in its own juice (reserve juice for use in topping and cake)
1 teaspoon maple flavoring
⅓ cup plus 1 tablespoon xylitol
12-15 fresh cherries, halved with pits removed

Cake:
2 cups whole wheat pastry flour
2 teaspoons baking soda
½ teaspoon salt
4 tablespoons unsalted butter, melted
¼ cup unsweetened applesauce
1 cup reduced-fat sour cream
1 teaspoon vanilla extract
1 teaspoon maple flavoring
2 eggs, separated
1⅓ cups xylitol

Prepare pan: Butter a 9" x 13" baking pan, line bottom and 1" up the sides of pan with parchment paper, and butter the parchment paper.

To prepare topping: In small saucepan, melt butter; stir in ¼ cup of the reserved pineapple juice, maple flavoring, and xylitol. Pour mixture into prepared pan, tilting it so that liquid covers entire bottom of pan. Arrange pineapple slices in pan, and place cherry halves (rounded side down) in center of and between each pineapple slice. Set pan aside while preparing cake.

To prepare cake batter: Combine flour, baking soda, and salt in a medium bowl and set aside. In another bowl, mix together melted butter, applesauce, sour cream, vanilla extract, maple flavoring, egg yolks, and remaining ½ cup of reserved

Continued on next page

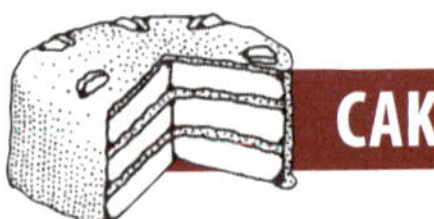

Pineapple Upside-down Cake

Continued from previous page

pineapple juice. In a large bowl, beat egg whites with mixer until soft peaks form; gradually add xylitol and beat until peaks are stiff but not dry. Using a spatula, gradually fold dry ingredients into beaten egg whites alternately with liquid ingredients, and stir just until batter is smooth. Gently spoon batter over pineapples and cherries in pan. Bake at 350° for 25-30 minutes or until toothpick inserted in center comes out clean. Remove from oven, place serving plate over cake, and immediately invert cake onto plate and serve warm.
Yield: 24 servings

Note: Fresh cherries are recommended in this recipe because the juice from frozen or canned cherries causes the surrounding cake to turn red, and looks unattractive. If desired, pecan halves may be used instead of, or even in addition to, the cherries.

Per Serving: **Calories:** 125.5 **Carbs:** 22.4g **Fiber:** 1.0g
Fat: 5.3g **Sodium:** 166.8mg **Net Carbs:** 9.3g

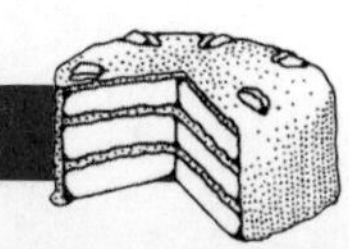

Spongecake

5 eggs, separated
½ teaspoon salt
½ teaspoon cream of tartar
1 cup xylitol, divided
1½ teaspoons grated lemon zest
1½ tablespoons freshly squeezed lemon juice
2 tablespoons water
¾ cup plus 2 tablespoons whole wheat pastry flour

In a large mixing bowl, beat egg whites and salt until foamy. Add cream of tartar, and continue beating until soft peaks form. Gradually beat ½ cup xylitol into egg whites, and beat until peaks are stiff but not dry; set aside. In separate bowl, beat egg yolks until well blended. Gradually beat remaining ½ cup xylitol into egg yolks. Combine lemon zest, lemon juice, and water; gradually add to egg yolks, and beat until light and fluffy. Fold flour into egg yolk mixture with a spatula until all ingredients are just blended, then fold this mixture into beaten egg whites until no streaks of yellow or white are visible.

Spoon into *ungreased* tube pan and gently smooth top of batter. Bake at 350° for 30-35 minutes or until toothpick inserted in center comes out clean. After removing cake from oven, *immediately* invert cake onto funnel or bottle, and allow it to cool completely before turning it right side up again. Remove from pan; slice with a serrated knife. **Yield: 16 servings**

Per Serving: **Calories:** 66.9 **Carbs:** 14.6g **Fiber:** 0.5g
Fat: 1.6g **Sodium:** 94.7mg **Net Carbs:** 3.6g

Pies

Apple Crisp

6 cups thinly sliced apples
1 cup quick-cooking oats, uncooked
¼ cup spelt flour or whole wheat pastry flour
½ teaspoon cinnamon
½ cup xylitol
¼ teaspoon maple flavoring
6 tablespoons unsalted butter
¼ cup chopped pecans

Place apple slices in a buttered 9" square baking pan. Combine oats, flour, cinnamon, xylitol, and maple flavoring. Cut in butter until mixture is crumbly, and spoon over apples. Bake at 350° for 40-45 minutes or until apples can be easily pierced with a knife and topping is golden brown. *Do not allow topping to darken as this will result in a bitter taste.*
Yield: 12 servings

Per Serving: **Calories:** 150.2 **Carbs:** 21.9g **Fiber:** 2.7g
Fat: 8.1g **Sodium:** 1.1mg **Net Carbs:** 12.2g

Apple Pie with Streusel Topping

Apple Filling:
8 cups thinly sliced apples
1 tablespoon freshly squeezed lemon juice
½ cup xylitol
1 tablespoon arrowroot powder (use additional ½ tablespoon if apples are very juicy.)
⅛ teaspoon salt
½ teaspoon grated lemon zest
¼ teaspoon nutmeg
1 teaspoon cinnamon
1 tablespoon unsalted butter
10″ pie crust, p. 39

Streusel Topping:
⅓ cup xylitol
⅔ cup spelt flour or whole wheat pastry flour
½ cup chopped pecans
1 teaspoon cinnamon
4½ tablespoons unsalted butter
1 teaspoon vanilla extract
¼ teaspoon maple flavoring

To make apple filling: Place apple slices in large bowl, and stir in lemon juice. Mix xylitol, arrowroot powder, salt, lemon zest, nutmeg, and cinnamon and sprinkle over apples. Stir well to evenly distribute cinnamon mixture. Place sweetened apple mixture in pie crust; dot with butter.

To make streusel topping: Combine xylitol, flour, pecans, and cinnamon. Stir in vanilla extract and maple flavoring. Cut in butter until crumbly. Sprinkle topping over apples.

Make a tent with foil and cover pie, cut several slits in foil for steam to escape, and bake at 425° for 1 hour. Reduce oven temperature to 400°, remove foil, and bake another 20 minutes or until apples can be easily pierced with a knife and juices are bubbling. **Yield: 12 servings**

Per Serving: **Calories:** 275.8 **Carbs:** 37.1g **Fiber:** 4.7g
Fat: 15.7g **Sodium:** 123mg **Net Carbs:** 20.7g

Blackberry Cobbler

4 cups blackberries
2 teaspoons lemon juice
½ cup xylitol
2 tablespoons arrowroot powder
⅛ teaspoon salt
1 tablespoon unsalted butter
Recipe for 9" pie crust, p. 38
2 teaspoons fat-free milk
2 teaspoons xylitol

Place blackberries in a buttered 8" square baking dish. Sprinkle with lemon juice. Combine ½ cup xylitol, arrowroot powder, and salt, and sprinkle mixture over berries. Dot with butter. Roll pastry out 1/8" thick; trim pastry dough to fit an 8" square baking pan. Place pastry over berries, and seal edges to sides of dish. Cut several 1" long slits in pastry. Brush pastry with milk, and sprinkle with 2 teaspoons xylitol. Bake at 425° for 30 minutes or until crust is golden brown. **Yield: 9 servings**

Per Serving: **Calories:** 177.1 **Carbs:** 26.9g **Fiber:** 4.9g
Fat: 8.8g **Sodium:** 138.6mg **Net Carbs:** 11.9g

Blueberry Cobbler

½ cup xylitol
2 tablespoons arrowroot powder
¼ teaspoon cinnamon
¼ teaspoon nutmeg
4½ cups fresh or frozen blueberries
1 tablespoon freshly squeezed lemon juice
1 tablespoon unsalted butter
Recipe for 9" pie crust, p. 38

Combine xylitol, arrowroot, cinnamon, and nutmeg; add blueberries, stirring until coated. Spoon blueberry mixture into a buttered 8" square baking dish. Sprinkle lemon juice over berries, and dot with butter. Roll pastry out 1/8" thick; trim pastry dough to fit an 8" square baking pan. Place pastry over blueberries, and seal edges to sides of dish. Cut several 1" long slits in pastry. Bake at 375° for 25-30 minutes or until pastry is golden brown. **Yield: 9 servings**

Per Serving: **Calories:** 189.2 **Carbs:** 30.5g **Fiber:** 3.3g
Fat: 8.8g **Sodium:** 105.8mg **Net Carbs:** 17.9g

Chocolate Chiffon Pie

1⅓ cups fat-free milk
1 envelope unflavored gelatin
1⅓ cups xylitol, divided
½ teaspoon salt
3 eggs, separated
2 ounces unsweetened chocolate bar, broken into small pieces
1 teaspoon vanilla extract
¼ teaspoon cream of tartar
9" baked pie crust, p. 38

Place milk in a small saucepan and heat to almost boiling. Remove from heat and set aside. Combine gelatin, ¾ cup xylitol, and salt in a medium bowl. Beat egg yolks into xylitol mixture and gradually stir in scalded milk. Transfer this mixture to top of double boiler, add chocolate pieces and cook over boiling water, stirring constantly, until chocolate melts and mixture begins to thicken. Remove from heat, and stir in vanilla extract. Transfer chocolate mixture to a bowl and refrigerate for one hour, stirring occasionally.

Beat egg whites and cream of tartar until foamy. Gradually add remaining xylitol (½ cup plus 4 teaspoons), and beat until peaks are stiff but not dry. Fold beaten egg whites into chocolate mixture, and pour filling into prepared pie crust. Refrigerate several hours before serving. **Yield: 8 servings**

Note: If desired, 2 tablespoons of powdered egg whites mixed in 6 tablespoons of water may be substituted for the egg whites.

Per Serving: **Calories:** 263.1 **Carbs:** 41.6g **Fiber:** 2.6g
Fat: 13.4g **Sodium:** 305.8mg **Net Carbs:** 11g

Chocolate Pecan Pie

3 tablespoons unsalted butter
¾ cup plus 3 tablespoons xylitol
¼ teaspoon salt
2 teaspoons vanilla extract
1 teaspoon maple flavoring
3 eggs, slightly beaten
2 ½ ounces xylitol-sweetened dark chocolate bar, finely chopped
¾ cup pecans, finely chopped
9" piecrust, p.38

If desired, pie shell can be pre-baked while filling is being prepared (see page xi). Reduce oven temperature to 275° when pie shell is removed from oven.

Melt butter in saucepan over low heat. Stir in xylitol, salt, and flavorings. Remove from heat and add eggs; stir well to combine. Cook over very low heat, stirring frequently until mixture is shiny and hot to touch. Do not allow mixture to simmer or boil. Stir in pecans and chocolate. Pour hot filling into hot pie shell and bake at 275° for 25-30 minutes. Allow pie to cool for 3-4 hours before serving.
Yield: 12 servings.

Per Serving: Calories: 266.8 **Carbs:** 27.8g **Fiber:** 2.6g
Fat: 19.8g **Sodium:** 165.4mg **Net Carbs:** 8.0g

Coconut Chess Pie

3 eggs, lightly beaten
1⅓ cups xylitol
1 tablespoon arrowroot powder
1/8 teaspoon salt
1 cup shredded unsweetened coconut
6 tablespoons plain low-fat yogurt
1 tablespoon water
1 tablespoon freshly squeezed lemon juice
4 tablespoons unsalted butter, melted
1 tablespoon unsweetened applesauce
1 teaspoon vanilla extract
¼ teaspoon butter flavoring
9" pie crust, p. 38

Combine xylitol, arrowroot powder, and salt; lightly beat into eggs. Mix in remaining ingredients in order given until well incorporated. Pour into pie crust and bake at 350° for 40 minutes; cover pie with aluminum foil and bake another 10 minutes. **Yield: 8 servings**

Per Serving: **Calories:** 339.2 **Carbs:** 42g **Fiber:** 3.2g
Fat: 22g **Sodium:** 185.4mg **Net Carbs:** 10.9g

Holiday Cranberry Walnut Cobbler

Filling:
4 cups fresh cranberries (two 8-oz. packages)
1⅓ cups xylitol
¾ cup coarsely chopped walnuts
3 tablespoons freshly squeezed orange juice
2 teaspoons cornstarch
⅓ cup unsalted butter

Batter:
¼ cup xylitol
1 cup spelt flour or whole wheat pastry flour
2 teaspoons baking powder
1 egg
½ cup low-fat milk

To prepare filling: In a large bowl combine xylitol with cranberries that have been cut in half. (Cutting cranberries in half prevents them from bursting during baking, which helps them to retain their shape.) Stir well to coat all the berries with xylitol. Cover and set aside for two hours or place in refrigerator overnight. After allowing mixture to sit, add walnuts. In small bowl, stir orange juice into cornstarch and add to filling. Melt butter and pour into 8" square baking pan. Spoon filling over melted butter in baking pan.

To prepare batter: Combine xylitol with flour and baking powder. Add egg and milk, and mix well. Pour batter over filling, and bake at 350° for 30-35 minutes or until crust is lightly browned. Best when served warm. **Yield: 9 servings**

Per Serving: **Calories:** 273.4 **Carbs:** 45.8g **Fiber:** 3.9g
Fat: 14.2g **Sodium:** 97.6mg **Net Carbs:** 12.4g

Key Lime Pie

1 recipe Sweetened Condensed Milk, p. 104
4 egg yolks
⅔ cup freshly squeezed lime juice
1 teaspoon finely grated lime zest
1 recipe Italian Meringue, p. 37
9" graham cracker crust, page 39

In a medium bowl, whisk together sweetened condensed milk and egg yolks. Gradually beat in lime juice and zest. Gently fold 1 cup of meringue into lime filling, and pour into pie crust. Bake at 350° for 15 minutes. Remove from oven and spread remaining meringue over filling, and seal meringue to edge of pastry. Bake at 350° for 5 minutes, and then broil briefly until meringue is light golden. Cool at room temperature for 30 minutes, then refrigerate for at least 4 hours before serving. **Yield: 10 servings**

Per Serving: **Calories:** 258.5 **Carbs:** 43.5g **Fiber:** 0.4g
Fat: 11.6g **Sodium:** 146.6mg **Net Carbs:** 14.9g

Lemon Ice Box Pie

Follow directions for Key Lime Pie, except substitute lemon juice and lemon zest instead of lime juice and lime zest.

Per Serving: **Calories:** 258.5 **Carbs:** 43.6g **Fiber:** 0.4g
Fat: 11.6g **Sodium:** 146.5mg **Net Carbs:** 14.9g

Magnolia Pie

3 eggs
3 tablespoons unsalted butter, melted
1 cup xylitol
2 tablespoons arrowroot powder
1 cup plus 2 tablespoons plain whole milk yogurt
1 teaspoon vanilla extract
½ teaspoon lemon extract
1 teaspoon finely grated lemon zest
9" pie crust, page 38

Beat eggs and butter until well blended. Add xylitol, arrowroot powder, yogurt, vanilla extract, lemon extract, and lemon zest and mix until smooth. Pour into pie crust and bake at 325° for 1 hour or until knife inserted in center comes out clean. **Yield: 10 servings**

Per Serving: **Calories:** 206.6 **Carbs:** 27.2g **Fiber:** 1.3g
Fat: 11.9g **Sodium:** 122.3mg **Net Carbs:** 9.1g

Peanut Butter Pie Squares

8 ounces reduced-fat cream cheese
12 ounces extra-firm silken tofu
½ cup xylitol
1 teaspoon vanilla extract
½ cup plus 1 tablespoon peanut butter
Recipe for 9" baked graham cracker crust, p. 39

To prepare crust: Use recipe for 9" graham cracker crust, and press mixture onto bottom and 1" up the sides of an 8" square baking pan. Bake at 350° for 8 minutes.

To prepare filling: Place cream cheese and tofu together in food processor or blender, and process until mixture is very smooth. Add xylitol, vanilla extract, and peanut butter, and process again until all ingredients are thoroughly combined. Pour mixture into crust. Refrigerate for several hours or overnight before serving. **Yield: 16 servings**

Per Serving: **Calories:** 169.5 **Carbs:** 14.9g **Fiber:** 0.7g
Fat: 11.4g **Sodium:** 151.3mg **Net Carbs:** 6.9g

Pecan Pie Squares

Recipe for 9" pie crust, p. 38
4 egg yolks
4 tablespoons unsalted butter
¾ cup plus 2 tablespoons xylitol
2 tablespoons reduced-fat sour cream
2 tablespoons plain whole milk yogurt
¼ teaspoon salt
1 teaspoon vanilla extract
½ teaspoon maple flavoring
1 cup pecan halves
¼ cup finely chopped pecans

To prepare pastry: Use recipe for 9" pie crust, but roll and cut dough to cover bottom and 1" up sides of 8" square baking pan. Pre-bake crust as directed on page xi.

To prepare filling: Place the pecans, flat sides down, on bottom of pie crust. In a saucepan, combine the egg yolks, butter, xylitol, sour cream, yogurt, and salt. Cook over low heat, stirring constantly, for 8-10 minutes or until mixture begins to thicken. Stir in vanilla extract, maple flavoring, and finely chopped pecans. Pour filling over pecans in pie crust, and bake at 350° for 20-25 minutes or until filling puffs up and begins to bubble around edges. Allow pie to cool completely before serving. **Yield: 16 servings**

Per Serving: **Calories:** 176 **Carbs:** 15.3g **Fiber:** 1.5g
Fat: 13.7g **Sodium:** 96mg **Net Carbs:** 4.7g

Pumpkin Chiffon Pie

2 eggs, lightly beaten
1¾ cups canned pumpkin (substitute pureed butternut squash, if desired)
¾ cup plus 3 tablespoons xylitol, divided
⅛ teaspoon salt
⅛ teaspoon cloves
¼ teaspoon ginger
¼ teaspoon nutmeg
1½ teaspoons cinnamon
¾ cup evaporated skim milk
2 tablespoons unsalted butter, melted
3 teaspoons gelatin (1½ envelopes)
4 teaspoons powdered egg whites
¼ teaspoon vanilla extract
Pecan Crunch Graham Cracker Crust, page 40

In large mixing bowl, combine eggs and pumpkin and mix well. Combine ¾ cup xylitol, salt, and spices and blend into pumpkin mixture. Gradually stir in evaporated milk and melted butter. Transfer this mixture to a double boiler, and cook until thickened into a custard; remove from heat. Dissolve gelatin in 6 tablespoons water, and stir into custard. Transfer to a large bowl and refrigerate until cool.

Whisk powdered egg whites with ¼ cup water for several minutes or until powder is dissolved. Beat egg whites with small mixer until soft peaks form. Gradually add 3 tablespoons xylitol and vanilla extract, and continue to beat until peaks are stiff but not dry. Gently fold beaten egg whites into custard. Pour filling into pie crust and refrigerate for several hours or preferably overnight. **Yield: 10 servings**

Note: Pureed butternut squash makes a delicious pie that tastes just like pumpkin, and no one will know the difference!

Per Serving: **Calories:** 215.3 **Carbs:** 32.6g **Fiber:** 2g
Fat: 10.6g **Sodium:** 245.7mg **Net Carbs:** 12.7g

Pumpkin Pie

2 eggs
1¾ cups canned pumpkin
¾ cup xylitol
⅛ teaspoon salt
⅛ teaspoon cloves
¼ teaspoon ginger
¼ teaspoon nutmeg
1½ teaspoons cinnamon
¾ cup evaporated skim milk
2 tablespoons unsalted butter, melted
9" pie crust, page 38

In large mixing bowl, lightly beat eggs. Add pumpkin and mix well. Combine xylitol, salt, and spices and blend into pumpkin mixture; gradually stir in evaporated milk and melted butter. Pour filling into pie crust. Bake at 375° for 50-60 minutes, or until knife inserted in center comes out clean. Serve chilled and topped with whipped cream and a sprinkle of cinnamon. **Yield: 8 servings**

Note: Mixing the pumpkin filling in the food processor creates an exceptionally smooth and silky texture.

Per Serving: **Calories:** 232.7 **Carbs:** 32.7g **Fiber:** 3.3g
Fat: 11.9g **Sodium:** 321.3mg **Net Carbs:** 13.6g

Southern Sweet Potato Cream Pie

3 cups cooked, mashed sweet potatoes
3 tablespoons unsalted butter, melted
½ cup plus 2 tablespoons xylitol
1 teaspoon cinnamon
¾ teaspoon nutmeg
½ teaspoon lemon extract
1½ teaspoons vanilla extract
3 eggs
¾ cup evaporated skim milk
10" pie crust, p. 39

In a large bowl, combine sweet potatoes, butter, xylitol, spices, lemon extract, vanilla extract, and eggs, and beat until mixture is smooth. Gradually add evaporated milk to sweet potato mixture, beating until well blended. Pour filling into pie crust. Bake at 375° for 40 minutes or until knife inserted in center comes out clean. Allow pie to cool completely before serving. **Yield: 10 servings**

Per Serving: **Calories:** 295 **Carbs:** 41g **Fiber:** 3.1g
Fat: 13.4g **Sodium:** 219.9mg **Net Carbs:** 27.5g

Italian Meringue

½ cup xylitol
2 tablespoons water
4 egg whites
½ teaspoon cream of tartar

In a small nonstick saucepan, combine xylitol and water and stir well. Cook over medium heat, stirring constantly, until xylitol dissolves and mixture bubbles. Remove from heat. In a large bowl, beat egg whites until foamy. Add cream of tartar and beat until stiff peaks form. Return saucepan to heat, and cook to 236°F. (soft ball stage). Immediately begin pouring mixture in a steady stream into beaten egg whites while beating, and continue beating until bowl is no longer hot and stiff peaks are formed. Spread meringue over pie filling, and bake at 350° for 5 minutes, then broil briefly until meringue is light golden.

For One Recipe: **Calories:** 273.7 **Carbs:** 85.7g
Fiber: 0g **Fat:** 0.2g **Sodium:** 220.5mg **Net Carbs:** 1.9g

Pie Crust – 9"

1 cup spelt flour or whole wheat pastry flour
3/8 teaspoon salt
5 tablespoons unsalted butter, cut into small pieces
1-3 tablespoons ice water

Hand Mixing: Combine flour and salt in large bowl. Cut butter in until mixture is texture of coarse meal. Sprinkle 1 tablespoon of water at a time over flour mixture, and mix lightly with a fork after each addition until pastry is just moist enough to hold together when pressed between fingers. Shape the pastry into a flattened disc, cover with plastic wrap, and chill for 30 minutes. Roll pastry between two sheets of wax paper until pastry is desired size. Refrigerate briefly; remove wax paper and fit pastry into pie plate.

Food Processor Method: Place flour and salt in food processor. Using the metal blade, pulse on and off a few times to combine mixture well. Remove lid and distribute pieces of butter evenly into container. Replace lid, and pulse several times or until texture of mixture resembles coarse meal. Add 1 tablespoon of water at a time through feed tube, pulse several times after each addition until pastry holds together when pressed between fingers. Continue to prepare pastry as described above.

Note: See page xi for baking information.

For a 9" Crust: **Calories:** 899.1 **Carbs:** 75g **Fiber:** 12g
Fat: 60.6g **Sodium:** 880.5mg **Net Carbs:** 63g

Pie Crust – 10"

1⅓ cups spelt flour or whole wheat pastry flour
½ teaspoon salt
6 tablespoons plus 2 teaspoons unsalted butter
2-3 tablespoons ice water

Follow directions for preparing 9" pie crust.

For a 10" Crust: **Calories:** 1198.2 **Carbs:** 100.1g
Fiber: 16g **Fat:** 80.7g **Sodium:** 1174mg **Net Carbs:** 84.1g

Graham Cracker Crust

1¼ cups graham cracker crumbs
(1 individually wrapped package)
3 tablespoons xylitol
3½ tablespoons unsalted butter, melted

To prepare 9" crust: Combine graham cracker crumbs and xylitol; stir in melted butter. Press mixture evenly into pie plate and bake at 350° for 8 minutes.

For a 9" Crust: **Calories:** 876 **Carbs:** 112.1g
Fiber: 2.9g **Fat:** 50.9g **Sodium:** 640.7mg **Net Carbs:** 77.7g

---

To prepare 10" crust: Increase the graham cracker crumbs to 1½ cups, the xylitol to ¼ cup, and the butter to 4 tablespoons.

For a 10" Crust: **Calories:** 1040.8 **Carbs:** 138.7g
Fiber: 3.5g **Fat:** 58.8g **Sodium:** 768.5mg **Net Carbs:** 93.3g

Chocolate Graham Cracker Crust

1¼ cups graham cracker crumbs
⅓ cup xylitol
4 tablespoons unsweetened cocoa powder, sifted
⅓ cup unsalted butter, melted

Combine graham cracker crumbs, xylitol, and cocoa powder; stir in melted butter. Press mixture evenly into 9" pie plate. Bake at 350° for 7-8 minutes. Allow crust to cool completely before filling.

For a 9" Crust: **Calories:** 1170.3 **Carbs:** 148.3g
Fiber: 10.1g **Fat:** 74.9g **Sodium:** 648.1mg **Net Carbs:** 82.3g

Pecan Crunch Graham Cracker Crust

1¼ cups graham cracker crumbs
(1 individually wrapped package)
¼ cup finely chopped pecans
2 tablespoons xylitol
⅛ teaspoon cinnamon
3½ tablespoons unsalted butter, melted
1 tablespoon unsweetened applesauce

Combine graham cracker crumbs, pecans, xylitol, and cinnamon; stir in melted butter and applesauce. Press mixture evenly into 10" pie plate and bake at 350° for 8 minutes.

For a 10" Crust: **Calories:** 1046.4 **Carbs:** 107.4g
Fiber: 5.9g **Fat:** 70.5g **Sodium:** 641.1mg **Net Carbs:** 80.5g

Cheesecakes

Almond-flavored Cheesecake

Crust:
5 tablespoons unsalted butter, softened
4½ tablespoons xylitol
1 cup spelt flour or whole wheat pastry flour
¼ teaspoon salt
¼ cup finely chopped pecans

Filling:
12 ounces low-fat cottage cheese
2 (8 oz.) packages reduced-fat cream cheese, softened
¾ cup xylitol
3 eggs
¾ teaspoon vanilla extract
¾ teaspoon almond extract
1 cup reduced-fat sour cream
1 cup low-fat plain yogurt

To prepare crust: Cream butter and xylitol together until light and fluffy. Stir in flour, salt, and pecans. Lightly butter bottom of 9" springform pan. Cut parchment paper to fit bottom of pan only, and place in pan. Press half of dough onto bottom of pan (sides removed). Bake at 350° for 10-12 minutes, or until very light golden. Remove from oven, and allow to cool completely. Attach sides to pan, and attach remaining dough from bottom 1" up sides of pan.

To prepare filling: Process cottage cheese in blender or food processor until smooth and creamy. Beat cream cheese and xylitol together until light and fluffy; blend in creamed cottage cheese. Add eggs, one at a time, beating until just blended. Stir in extracts. Combine sour cream and yogurt; gently fold into cream cheese mixture.

Variation: Pour half of cheesecake batter into pan. Using ½ cup of pureed strawberries, blueberries, or raspberries, ran-

Continued on next page

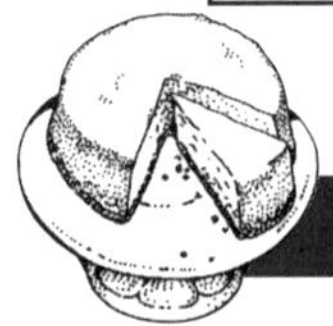

Almond-flavored Cheesecake

Continued from previous page

domly drop spoonfuls of the puree over the batter. Then top with remaining cheesecake batter. Draw a knife through the batter several times to create a marbled effect. Bake as directed below. **Yield: 16 servings**

Per Serving: **Calories:** 234 **Carbs:** 19.4g **Fiber:** 0.9g
Fat: 15.2g **Sodium:** 270.6mg **Net Carbs:** 7.6g

To Bake Cheesecake

Pour into springform pan, bake in water bath (see page xii) at 325° for 50 minutes. Turn oven off, prop oven door open slightly, and leave cheesecake in oven another 30 minutes. Remove cheesecake from water bath, allow it to sit at room temperature for 30 minutes, then refrigerate for at least 8 hours. Carefully remove sides of pan, loosen cheesecake from bottom of pan, and slide cheesecake onto a serving plate.

Cherry Cheesecake

Almond Pastry:
5 tablespoons unsalted butter, softened
5 tablespoons xylitol
1 cup spelt flour or whole wheat pastry flour
¼ teaspoon salt
¼ cup ground almonds

Filling:
12 ounces low-fat cottage cheese
2 (8 oz.) packages reduced-fat cream cheese, softened
1 cup xylitol
⅛ teaspoon salt
3 eggs
1¾ teaspoons cherry flavoring
⅓ cup low-fat plain yogurt
⅓ cup reduced-fat sour cream
⅓ cup finely chopped dried cherries
that have mascerated in 3 tablespoons cherry liqueur
for 1 hour or until cherries have absorbed all the liqueur

To prepare crust: Cream together butter and xylitol until light and fluffy. Stir in flour, salt, and almonds. Lightly butter bottom of 9" springform pan. Cut parchment paper to fit bottom of pan only. Press half of dough onto bottom of pan (sides removed). Bake at 350° for 10-12 minutes or until very light golden. Remove from oven, and allow to cool completely. Attach sides to bottom of pan, and press remaining dough from bottom of pan 1" up sides of pan.

To prepare filling: Process cottage cheese in blender or food processor until smooth and creamy. Beat cream cheese and xylitol until light and fluffy; blend in creamed cottage cheese and salt. Add eggs, one at a time, beating until just blended. Gently fold in yogurt, sour cream, and cherries. **Yield: 16 servings**

To bake cheesecake: See page 43.

Per Serving: **Calories:** 229 **Carbs:** 24g **Fiber:** 1.1g
Fat: 13.1g **Sodium:** 276mg **Net Carbs:** 9.2g

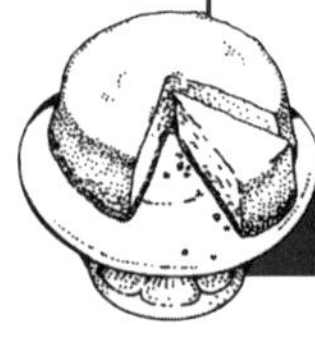

Grasshopper Cheesecake

Crust:
1¼ cups graham cracker crumbs
⅓ cup xylitol
4 tablespoons unsweetened cocoa powder, sifted
⅓ cup unsalted butter, melted

Filling:
12 ounces low-fat cottage cheese
2 (8 oz.) packages reduced-fat cream cheese, softened
¾ cup plus 2 tablespoons xylitol
3 eggs
2½ tablespoons crème de cacao
2½ tablespoons crème de menthe
1½ teaspoons vanilla extract
⅓ cup plain low-fat yogurt
⅓ cup reduced-fat sour cream

To prepare crust: Lightly butter bottom of 9" springform pan. Cut parchment paper to fit bottom of pan only, and place in pan. Combine graham cracker crumbs, xylitol, cocoa powder; stir in melted butter. Press mixture onto bottom and 1" up sides of 9" springform pan. Bake at 350° for 7–8 minutes. Allow crust to cool completely before adding filling.

To prepare filling: Process cottage cheese in blender or food processor until smooth and creamy. Beat cream cheese and xylitol until light and fluffy; blend in creamed cottage cheese. Add eggs, one at a time, beating until just blended. Combine liqueurs and vanilla extract, and stir into filling. Combine yogurt and sour cream and gently fold into cream cheese mixture. **Yield: 16 servings**

To bake cheesecake: See page 43.

Per Serving: **Calories:** 229 **Carbs:** 23g **Fiber:** 0.6g
Fat: 13.3g **Sodium:** 260.3mg **Net Carbs:** 9.6g

Lemon Cheesecake

Crust:
5 tablespoons unsalted butter, softened
¼ cup xylitol
1 cup spelt flour or whole wheat pastry flour
¼ teaspoon salt
1 teaspoon grated lemon zest

Filling:
12 ounces low-fat cottage cheese
2 (8 oz.) packages reduced-fat cream cheese, softened
1 cup xylitol
⅛ teaspoon salt
3 eggs
½ teaspoon lemon extract
1 teaspoon finely grated lemon zest
⅓ cup low-fat plain yogurt
⅓ cup reduced-fat sour cream

To prepare crust: Cream butter and xylitol together until light and fluffy. Stir in flour, salt, and lemon zest. Lightly butter bottom of 9" springform pan. Cut parchment paper to fit bottom of pan only, and place in pan. Press half of dough evenly in bottom of pan (sides removed). Bake at 350° for 10-12 minutes, or until very light golden. Remove from oven, and allow to cool completely. Attach sides to pan, and attach remaining dough from bottom 1" up sides of pan.

To prepare filling: Process cottage cheese in blender or food processor until smooth and creamy. Beat cream cheese and xylitol together until light and fluffy; blend in creamed cottage cheese and salt. Add eggs, one at a time, beating until just blended. Stir in lemon extract and lemon zest; mix well. Combine yogurt and sour cream; gently fold into cream cheese mixture. **Yield: 16 servings**

To bake cheesecake: See page 43.

Per Serving: **Calories:** 202.8 **Carbs:** 20g **Fiber:** 0.8g
Fat: 12.4g **Sodium:** 274.6mg **Net Carbs:** 6.1g

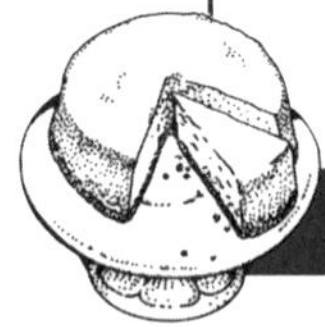

Orange Cheesecake

Crust:
1½ cups graham cracker crumbs
¼ cup xylitol
4 tablespoons unsalted butter, melted

Filling:
12 ounces low-fat cottage cheese
2 (8 oz.) packages reduced-fat cream cheese, softened
1 cup xylitol
3 eggs
1 tablespoon orange zest
2 tablespoons orange liqueur
¼ teaspoon orange extract
⅓ cup low-fat plain yogurt
⅓ cup reduced-fat sour cream

To prepare crust: Lightly butter bottom of 9" springform pan. Cut parchment paper to fit bottom of pan only, and place in pan. Combine graham cracker crumbs and xylitol; stir in melted butter. Press graham cracker mixture onto bottom and 1" up sides of pan. Bake at 350° for 5 minutes. Remove from oven and allow to cool completely before filling.

To prepare filling: Process cottage cheese in blender or food processor until smooth and creamy. Beat cream cheese and xylitol until light and fluffy; blend in creamed cottage cheese. Add eggs, one at a time, beating until just blended. Stir in orange zest, liqueur, and extract. Combine yogurt and sour cream; gently fold into cream cheese mixture. **Yield: 16 servings**

To bake cheesecake: See page 43.

Per Serving: **Calories:** 210.6 **Carbs:** 21.7g **Fiber:** 0.3g
Fat: 12.2g **Sodium:** 267.6mg **Net Carbs:** 8.3g

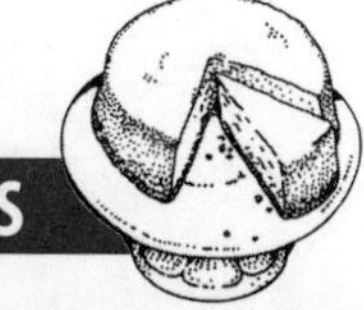

Pumpkin Cheesecake

Crust:
1½ cups graham cracker crumbs
¼ cup xylitol
4 tablespoons unsalted butter, melted

Filling:
12 ounces low-fat cottage cheese
2 (8 oz.) packages reduced-fat cream cheese, softened
¾ cup plus 2 tablespoons xylitol
3 eggs
1 egg yolk
½ teaspoon allspice
½ teaspoon ginger
½ teaspoon cinnamon
¼ teaspoon salt
1 cup plus 2 tablespoons canned pumpkin
⅓ cup reduced-fat sour cream
⅓ cup low-fat plain yogurt
1 teaspoon vanilla extract

To prepare crust: Lightly butter bottom of 9" springform pan. Cut parchment paper to fit bottom of pan only, and place in pan. Combine graham cracker crumbs and xylitol; stir in melted butter. Press graham cracker mixture onto bottom and 1" up sides of pan. Bake at 350° for 5 minutes. Remove from oven, and allow to cool completely before filling.

To prepare filling: Process cottage cheese in blender or food processor until smooth and creamy. Beat cream cheese and xylitol until light and fluffy; blend in creamed cottage cheese. Add eggs, one at a time, beating until just blended. Combine allspice, ginger, cinnamon, and salt; add to cream cheese mixture and mix well. Add pumpkin, sour cream, yogurt, and vanilla extract; mix until well blended. **Yield: 16 servings**

To bake cheesecake: See page 43.

Per Serving: **Calories:** 212.7 **Carbs:** 21.6g **Fiber:** 0.8g
Fat: 12.6g **Sodium:** 346.1mg **Net Carbs:** 9.1g

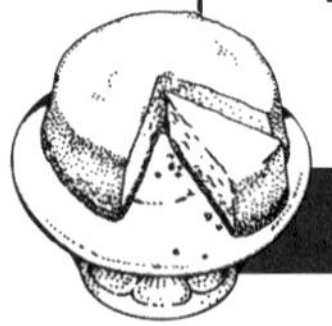

Cookies & Bars

Ambrosia Cream Cheese Cookies

Cookie Dough:
⅓ cup unsalted butter, softened
3 ounces reduced-fat cream cheese
2 tablespoons pureed orange*
1 cup xylitol
2 eggs
1½ teaspoons vanilla extract
2¼ cups spelt flour or whole wheat pastry flour
2 teaspoons baking powder
1 teaspoon baking soda
½ teaspoon salt
1 (8 ½ ounce) can crushed pineapple
(in its own juice), well drained
½ cup shredded unsweetened coconut
1 cup chopped pecans

Frosting:
1½ cups powdered xylitol, sifted
1½ teaspoon unsalted butter, softened
4 teaspoons pineapple juice
4 teaspoons freshly squeezed orange juice

To prepare cookie dough: Cream the butter and cream cheese together, and beat in pureed orange. Gradually add xylitol, beating until light and fluffy. Add eggs, one at a time, beating well after each addition. Stir in vanilla extract. Combine flour, baking powder, baking soda, and salt in a medium bowl and mix well. Gradually add dry ingredients to creamed mixture. Stir in pineapple, coconut, and pecans. Drop dough by rounded tablespoonfuls 2 inches apart onto parchment lined cookie sheet. Bake at 350° for 10-12 minutes or until cookies are very light golden.

Continued on next page

Ambrosia Cream Cheese Cookies

Continued from previous page

To prepare frosting: Combine all ingredients and beat until smooth. Spoon frosting over cooled cookies. **Yield: 3 dozen cookies**

***To prepare pureed orange:** Place ½ cup water and 1 small coarsely chopped Valencia orange in blender. Process briefly until mixture is smooth.

Per Cookie: **Calories:** 102 **Carbs:** 18.7g **Fiber:** 1.2g
Fat: 5.8g **Sodium:** 101.5mg **Net Carbs:** 8.6g

Apple Oatmeal Bars

Filling:
½ cup xylitol
1½ teaspoons cinnamon
½ teaspoon nutmeg
2 cups finely chopped apples (no need to peel apples)
1 tablespoon unsalted butter, melted

Crust:
1 cup spelt flour or whole wheat pastry flour
½ teaspoon baking soda
½ cup xylitol
½ teaspoon salt
1 cup quick-cooking oats, uncooked
4 tablespoons unsalted butter
3 tablespoons unsweetened applesauce
½ teaspoon maple flavoring

To prepare filling: Mix ½ cup xylitol, cinnamon, and nutmeg together; stir in apples and butter, and set aside while preparing crust.

To prepare crust: Combine flour, baking soda, ½ cup xylitol, salt, and oats. Cut in butter, and stir in applesauce and maple flavoring; mixture should be crumbly.

To prepare bars: Spoon half of crust mixture onto bottom of buttered 7½" x 12" baking dish, and gently press evenly into place. Spoon filling over crust, and sprinkle remaining crust mixture over apple filling. Bake at 350° for 30-35 minutes or until light golden brown. **Yield: 18 bars**

Per Bar: **Calories:** 98.4 **Carbs:** 18.8g **Fiber:** 1.6g
Fat: 3.7g **Sodium:** 100.4mg **Net Carbs:** 7.9g

Chocolate Chip Coconut Bars

1½ cups graham cracker crumbs
4 tablespoons unsalted butter
¼ cup xylitol
⅔ cup shredded unsweetened coconut
1 cup chopped pecans
1 recipe sweetened condensed milk (p. 104)
5 ounces xylitol-sweetened dark chocolate bars, chopped

Combine graham cracker crumbs, butter and xylitol; press onto bottom of buttered 9" x 13" pan. Bake at 350° for 8 minutes. Combine coconut, pecans, and sweetened condensed milk, and pour over crust. Sprinkle chocolate evenly over top of bars. Gently press chocolate onto filling using back of spoon. Bake at 350° for 20-25 minutes. Center will be soft, but will become more firm as bars cool. **Yield: 36 bars**

Per Bar: **Calories:** 113.7 **Carbs:** 13.2g **Fiber:** 1.1g
Fat: 8.2g **Sodium:** 39.2mg **Net Carbs:** 5.2g

Chocolate Chip Cookies

2 ¼ cups spelt flour or whole wheat pastry flour
1 teaspoon baking soda
1 teaspoon salt
12 ounces (2 cups) xylitol-sweetened dark chocolate bars, chopped
1 cup pecans, chopped
12 tablespoons unsalted butter (1 ½ sticks), melted
1 cup + 7 tablespoons xylitol
2 tablespoons unsweetened applesauce
2 teaspoons vanilla extract
2 teaspoons molasses flavoring (or 1 tablespoon molasses)
2 egg yolks

Place flour, baking soda, and salt in large bowl, stir well to combine; add chocolate and nuts, stir well to coat. In medium saucepan, melt butter and remove pan from heat; stir in xylitol, applesauce, flavorings, and egg yolks. Add the butter mixture to the flour mixture all at once and stir just until dry ingredients are moistened. Weigh out 40 one ounce cookies, roll into balls, and place in freezer on lined cookie sheet until frozen. Transfer cookie balls to zip-top bag and store in freezer until ready to bake. Bake frozen cookie balls on cookie sheet at 375°for 15-20 minutes or until golden brown, but still a little moist in center. When cookies are firm enough to move (2-3 minutes), transfer to a cooling rack. **Yield: 40 (one ounce) cookies.**

Per Cookie: **Calories:** 138 **Carbs:** 16g **Fiber:** 2g
Fat: 10.3g **Sodium:** 96.2mg **Net Carbs:** 6g

White Chocolate Macadamia Nut Cookies

Follow above directions for Chocolate Chip Cookies except: Substitute xylitol-sweetened white chocolate bars for the dark chocolate, and substitute ⅔ cup chopped macadamia nuts for the pecans. Allow cookies to cool a few minutes before removing them from the cookie sheet. Cool on wax paper. **Yield: 4 dozen cookies**

Per Cookie: **Calories:** 136.9 **Carbs:** 16.7g **Fiber:** 1.9g
Fat: 10.2g **Sodium:** 104.2mg **Net Carbs:** 6.1g

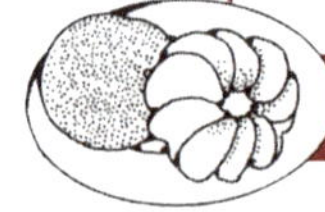

Chocolate Coconut Brownies

2 tablespoons unsalted butter
3 ounces unsweetened chocolate bar
1 cup plus 1 tablespoon xylitol
1½ teaspoons vanilla extract
3 eggs, beaten
¼ cup spelt flour or whole wheat pastry flour
⅓ cup shredded unsweetened coconut
⅓ cup chopped pecans

In saucepan over low heat, melt butter. Break chocolate bars into pieces and add to butter. Stir in xylitol and vanilla extract. Continue cooking over low heat, stirring frequently, until chocolate is completely melted. Remove from heat and stir in eggs until thoroughly combined with chocolate mixture. Stir in flour, coconut and pecans. Pour mixture into buttered 8" square pan and bake at 350° for 20-25 minutes or until outer edges are somewhat firm. Center will still be soft, but will become more firm as brownies cool. Allow brownies to cool completely before cutting. **Yield: 25 brownies**

Per Brownie: **Calories:** 73.7 **Carbs:** 9.4g **Fiber:** 1g
Fat: 5.2g **Sodium:** 9.4mg **Net Carbs:** 1.3g

Chocolate Cherry Brownies

Follow above directions for Chocolate Coconut Brownies except:

Delete the vanilla extract and substitute the same amount of cherry flavoring. Delete the coconut and the pecans. Soak 1/3 cup dried cherries in 3 tablespoons cherry liqueur for several hours or overnight. Drain excess liquid before adding cherries to the brownie batter. **Yield: 25 brownies**

Per Brownie: **Calories:** 66 **Carbs:** 10.9g **Fiber:** 0.7g
Fat: 3.4g **Sodium:** 9.9mg **Net Carbs:** 3g

Chocolate Pecan Bars

Crust:
1¼ cups spelt flour or whole wheat pastry flour
¼ cup plus 3 tablespoons xylitol
⅜ teaspoon salt
5 tablespoons unsalted butter
2½ tablespoons unsweetened applesauce
½ teaspoon maple flavoring

Filling:
1 cup plus 3 tablespoons xylitol
1½ cups dry milk powder
4 tablespoons unsalted butter
½ cup plus 2 tablespoons boiling water
1 egg
1½ teaspoons vanilla extract
½ teaspoon maple flavoring
1 teaspoon lecithin granules
½ cup unsweetened cocoa powder, sifted
1¾ cups chopped pecans

To make crust: Butter a 9" x 13" baking dish, line bottom and sides with parchment paper, and lightly butter parchment paper. Mix flour, xylitol, and salt together, then cut in butter until mixture resembles coarse crumbs. Stir in applesauce and maple flavoring; mixture will be crumbly. Press firmly onto bottom of prepared pan, and prick with fork halfway through crust. Bake at 350° for 15 minutes.

To make filling: Place xylitol, milk powder, butter, and boiling water in blender; process for several minutes or until mixture is smooth. Add egg, vanilla extract, maple flavoring, lecithin granules, and cocoa powder, and process again until smooth. Transfer to a large bowl, and stir in chopped pecans. Pour into baked crust, and bake at 350° for 20-25 minutes or just until filling is set. Allow to cool in pan before cutting into bars. **Yield: 48 bars**

Per Bar: **Calories:** 82.5 **Carbs:** 9.9g **Fiber:** 1g
Fat: 5.4g **Sodium:** 31.9mg **Net Carbs:** 3.2g

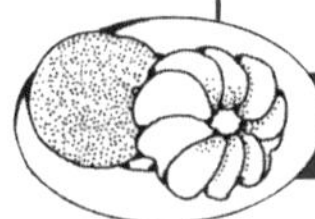

Chocolate Sandwich Cookies

4 tablespoons unsalted butter, softened
1 cup xylitol, plus extra xylitol for rolling cookies
¼ cup unsweetened applesauce
1 egg
1 teaspoon vanilla extract
1¼ cups spelt flour or whole wheat pastry flour
⅓ cup unsweetened cocoa powder, sifted
½ teaspoon baking soda
¼ teaspoon salt
1½ teaspoons lecithin granules

Cream butter and xylitol; gradually add applesauce during the creaming process. Beat in egg and vanilla extract. In another bowl combine flour, cocoa powder, baking soda, salt, and lecithin granules. Gradually add dry ingredients into creamed mixture until all ingredients are well mixed. Cover bowl and refrigerate for 2-3 hours or until dough can be handled easily. Shape dough into balls using ½ tablespoon of dough per cookie; roll in xylitol. Place on parchment lined cookie sheet, and flatten slightly with bottom of glass dipped in xylitol. Bake cookies at 350° for 10-12 minutes. Allow cookies to cool completely before putting together in pairs with one of the fillings listed on pages 69–72. **Yield: 2 dozen sandwich cookies**

Per Sandwich Cookie Without Filling: **Calories:** 62.2
Carbs: 11.9g **Fiber:** 1.1g **Fat:** 2.5g **Sodium:** 54mg
Net Carbs: 3.8g

Cranberry Bars

Filling:
1 cup plus 2 tablespoons xylitol
¾ cup water
3 cups fresh cranberries
¼ cup plus 2 tablespoons freshly squeezed orange juice
1½ tablespoons grated orange zest
1 tablespoons unsalted butter
¾ teaspoon cinnamon
⅜ teaspoon salt

Crust:
1¼ cups quick-cooking oats, uncooked
1¼ cups spelt flour or whole wheat pastry flour
¾ cup xylitol
⅔ cup finely chopped pecans
½ teaspoon salt
½ teaspoon baking soda
6 tablespoons unsalted butter, softened
1½ tablespoons unsweetened applesauce

To prepare filling: Combine xylitol and water in heavy saucepan and bring to a boil. Add cranberries and cook until cranberries pop, about 5 minutes. Stir in orange juice, orange zest, butter, cinnamon, and salt and cook another 5 minutes or until mixture thickens. Set aside to cool while preparing crust.

To prepare crust: Combine oats, flour, xylitol, pecans, salt, and baking soda; mix well. Cut in butter and stir in applesauce; mixture should be crumbly. Divide crust mixture in half; press half of mixture onto bottom of lightly buttered 9" x 13" baking pan. Bake at 375° for 10 minutes. Spread cooled filling over the crust, then sprinkle remaining crumb mixture over filling. Bake at 375° for 15-20 minutes or until light golden brown. **Yield: 32 bars**

Per Bar:	**Calories:** 93.7	**Carbs:** 16.5g	**Fiber:** 1.5g
Fat: 4.5g	**Sodium:** 84mg	**Net Carbs:** 5.2g	

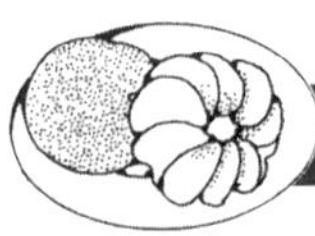

Date-filled Oatmeal Cookies

1¾ cups spelt flour or whole wheat pastry flour
3 cups quick-cooking oats, uncooked
1⅓ cups xylitol
1 teaspoon baking soda
½ teaspoon salt
½ teaspoon cinnamon
¼ teaspoon nutmeg
¼ teaspoon cloves
½ cup unsalted butter
¼ cup unsweetened applesauce
⅓ cup plus 1 tablespoon buttermilk
½ teaspoon maple flavoring

Filling:
1¼ cups chopped dates
¾ cup plus 2 tablespoons water
2½ tablespoons xylitol
4 teaspoons freshly squeezed lemon juice

To prepare cookie dough: Combine flour, oats, xylitol, baking soda, salt, cinnamon, nutmeg, and cloves; mix well. Cut in butter until mixture is crumbly. In small bowl combine applesauce, buttermilk, and maple flavoring; stir into dry ingredients. Shape dough into 4 rolls, 1½" in diameter. Wrap each roll in wax paper and refrigerate several hours or overnight.

To prepare filling: Combine all ingredients for filling in saucepan. Cook over medium heat, stirring constantly, until thick and smooth. If a smoother filling is desired, place cooked date mixture in food processor and process briefly. Allow filling to cool completely before preparing cookies.

To prepare cookies: Remove one roll of cookie dough at a time from refrigerator, and cut it into 1/8" thick slices. Place a slice onto parchment paper lined cookie sheet, place 1 teaspoon of date filling onto center of slice, and top with another slice of dough. Repeat process for remaining cookies. Bake at 350° for 10-12 minutes. **Yield: 3 dozen cookies**

Per Cookie: **Calories:** 104.2 **Carbs:** 20.2g **Fiber:** 1.8g
Fat: 3.2g **Sodium:** 70.5mg **Net Carbs:** 11.4g

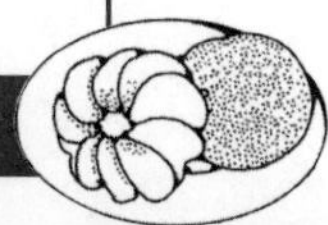

Double Chocolate Cherry Pecan Cookies

4 tablespoons unsalted butter
1½ ounces unsweetened chocolate bar, coarsely chopped
1 cup xylitol
4 tablespoons unsweetened applesauce
½ teaspoon maple flavoring
1 teaspoon vanilla extract
⅜ teaspoon cherry flavoring
1 egg
1 cup spelt flour or whole wheat pastry flour
¼ cup unsweetened cocoa powder, sifted
¾ teaspoon baking powder
¼ teaspoon baking soda
¼ teaspoon salt
1½ teaspoons lecithin granules
¾ cup chopped pecans
⅓ cup dried cherries (reconstituted and chopped)

In a saucepan, melt butter and chocolate bar over low heat, stirring frequently. Remove saucepan from heat and add xylitol, applesauce, maple flavoring, vanilla extract, cherry flavoring, and egg, stirring until well blended. In separate bowl combine flour, cocoa powder, baking powder, baking soda, salt, and lecithin granules and mix well. Gradually stir dry ingredients into butter mixture. Fold in pecans and cherries. Transfer cookie dough to a bowl, cover, and refrigerate 30 minutes for easier shaping. Drop dough by heaping teaspoonfuls 2 inches apart onto parchment lined cookie sheet. Bake at 350° for 8-10 minutes.
Yield: 4 ½ dozen cookies

Note: Watch cookies carefully toward the end of the baking time as they can quickly become overcooked. This recipe produces a satisfyingly rich and moist chocolate cookie.

Per Cookie: **Calories:** 42.7 **Carbs:** 6g **Fiber:** 0.7g
Fat: 2.6g **Sodium:** 23.7mg **Net Carbs:** 2.2g

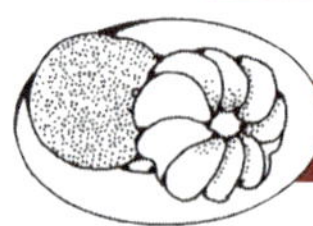

Easy Chocolate Brownie Squares

3 eggs
1 cup xylitol
¼ cup unsalted butter, melted
2 tablespoons unsweetened applesauce
⅓ cup cocoa powder, sifted
¼ cup spelt flour or whole wheat pastry flour
⅛ teaspoon salt
1 teaspoon vanilla extract
¼ teaspoon butter flavoring
⅔ cup pecans, coarsely chopped

Butter an 8" square baking pan, line bottom and 2 opposite sides with parchment paper, and lightly butter paper. In large bowl, beat 3 eggs and xylitol until fully incorporated. Add melted butter and applesauce, and stir well. Mix cocoa powder, flour, and salt together, and combine with egg mixture. Stir in vanilla extract, butter flavoring, and pecans. Spoon into pan and bake at 350° for 25-30 minutes, or until a toothpick inserted in center comes out clean. **Yield: 16 brownies**

Note: These brownies are similar to traditional cake brownies, and they stay fresh longer when cut and wrapped individually in plastic wrap and stored in an airtight container at room temperature.

Per Brownie Square: **Calories:** 107.6 **Carbs:** 13.6g
Fiber: 1.2g **Fat:** 7.4g **Sodium:** 32.1mg **Net Carbs:** 1.9g

Lemon Pecan Cookies

½ cup unsalted butter, softened
1 cup xylitol
¼ cup unsweetened applesauce
1 egg
1 tablespoon grated lemon zest
2 tablespoons freshly squeezed lemon juice
2 cups spelt flour or whole wheat pastry flour
½ teaspoon baking soda
⅜ teaspoon salt
½ cup finely chopped pecans

Cream butter and xylitol until light and fluffy; gradually add applesauce during creaming process. Beat in egg, lemon zest and juice. Combine flour, baking soda, salt, and pecans; gradually stir into creamed mixture. Roll into balls, using ½ tablespoon of dough per cookie. Place on parchment lined cookie sheet. Press down lightly with bottom of glass dipped in xylitol. Bake at 350° for 10-12 minutes or until underside of cookies is lightly brown. **Yield: 4 dozen cookies**

Note: These are really delicious when made into sandwich cookies using Lemon Filling, page 70.

Per Cookie: **Calories:** 51.7 **Carbs:** 7g **Fiber:** 0.6g
Fat: 3g **Sodium:** 33mg **Net Carbs:** 2.9g

Peanut Butter Cookies

4 tablespoons unsalted butter, softened
½ cup peanut butter
¾ cup xylitol
2 tablespoons unsweetened applesauce
¼ teaspoon maple flavoring
1 egg
½ teaspoon vanilla extract
1 cup plus 2 tablespoons oat flour
1 teaspoon baking soda
¼ teaspoon salt
⅓ cup chopped peanuts

Beat butter, peanut butter, and xylitol until well combined. Blend in applesauce, maple flavoring, egg, and vanilla extract. In small bowl, combine flour, baking soda, and salt. Gradually stir dry ingredients into peanut butter mixture; stir in peanuts. Cover and refrigerate overnight or until dough can be handled easily. Roll into balls, using ½ tablespoon of dough per cookie. Place on parchment lined cookie sheet. Flatten cookies with a fork dipped in xylitol to create a crisscross pattern. Bake at 350° for 8-10 minutes or until outer edges of cookies are light brown. **Yield: 4 dozen cookies.**

Note: Cookies are soft after baking, but will become more firm after they cool completely.

Per Cookie: **Calories:** 46.8 **Carbs:** 4.9g **Fiber:** 0.5g
Fat: 3.1g **Sodium:** 52.3mg **Net Carbs:** 1.8g

Pecan Balls

½ cup unsalted butter, softened
¼ cup powdered xylitol, sifted
1 teaspoon vanilla extract
1 tablespoon water
¼ cup unsweetened applesauce
2 cups spelt flour or whole wheat pastry flour
¼ teaspoon salt
2 cups very finely chopped pecans
Additional powdered xylitol for rolling balls after baking

Cream butter; mix in xylitol, vanilla extract, water, and applesauce. Stir in flour and salt. Stir in pecans and combine well. Refrigerate dough for 1 hour or until it can be handled easily. Shape dough into 1-inch balls. Place on parchment lined cookie sheet and bake at 350° for about 10-12 minutes or until bottom of cookies is very light golden. Remove from oven and immediately roll in powdered xylitol. **Yield: 5½ dozen pecan balls**

Per Ball: **Calories:** 48.4 **Carbs:** 3.6g **Fiber:** 0.7g
Fat: 3.9g **Sodium:** 9mg **Net Carbs:** 2.5g

Pumpkin Bars

Crust:
1¼ cups quick-cooking oats, uncooked
1¼ cups spelt flour or whole wheat pastry flour
¾ cup xylitol
¾ teaspoon maple flavoring
½ cup finely chopped pecans
½ teaspoon salt
½ teaspoon baking soda
6 tablespoons unsalted butter, softened
1½ tablespoons unsweetened applesauce

Filling:
2 cups canned pumpkin
1 egg
½ cup plus 2 tablespoons xylitol
1½ teaspoons cinnamon
¼ teaspoon ginger
¼ teaspoon nutmeg
¼ teaspoon allspice
⅛ teaspoon cloves
⅔ cup evaporated skim milk

To prepare crust: Combine oats, flour, xylitol, maple flavoring, pecans, salt, and baking soda; mix well. Cut in butter and stir in applesauce; mixture should be crumbly. Divide crust mixture in half; press half of mixture onto bottom of lightly buttered 9" x 13" baking pan. Bake at 375° for 10 minutes.

To prepare filling: Place all filling ingredients except milk in large bowl and mix well; stir in milk.

To prepare bars: Spread filling over the crust and then sprinkle remaining crumb mixture over filling. Bake at 375° for 18-20 minutes or until light golden brown. **Yield: 32 bars**

Per Bar: **Calories:** 88 **Carbs:** 14.6g **Fiber:** 1.5g
Fat: 3.9g **Sodium:** 101.7mg **Net Carbs:** 5.9g

Thumbprint Cookies

4 tablespoons unsalted butter, softened
⅓ cup xylitol
2 tablespoons unsweetened applesauce
1 egg yolk
½ teaspoon vanilla extract
1 cup spelt flour or whole wheat pastry flour
¼ teaspoon salt
½ cup finely chopped pecans
2 tablespoons fruit spread or jam of your choice

Cream butter and xylitol; gradually add applesauce during creaming process. Beat in egg yolk and vanilla extract. Combine flour and salt in a small bowl, and gradually stir into creamed mixture. Shape dough into ball, wrap in plastic wrap, and refrigerate for up to 1 hour or until dough is easily handled. Shape dough into 1-inch balls, and roll in chopped pecans. Place on a parchment lined cookie sheet, and press an indentation into each cookie using your thumb or a very small rounded measuring spoon. Fill each indentation with fruit spread. Bake at 375° for 10-12 minutes or until bottom of cookies are light brown. **Yield: 3 dozen cookies**

Note: These cookies taste delicious when filled with strawberry or raspberry jam.

Per Cookie: **Calories:** 39.4 **Carbs:** 4.3g **Fiber:** 0.5g
Fat: 2.6g **Sodium:** 16.5mg **Net Carbs:** 2g

Tropical Fruit Bars

Filling:
2 cups dates, chopped
20-ounce can crushed pineapple (in its own juice)

Crust:
1 cup spelt flour or whole wheat pastry flour
⅔ cup shredded unsweetened coconut
½ cup chopped pecans
3 cups quick-cooking oats, uncooked
¼ cup xylitol
1 tablespoon lecithin granules
1 cup freshly squeezed orange juice
2 tablespoons extra virgin olive oil
2 tablespoons unsweetened applesauce
½ teaspoon maple flavoring

To prepare filling: Combine the dates and pineapple with its juice in a saucepan. Cook on medium-low heat until fruit mixture is thick, stirring occasionally, and set aside to cool.

To prepare crust: In a large bowl, combine flour, coconut, pecans, oats, xylitol, and lecithin granules. In a small bowl, mix orange juice, olive oil, applesauce, and maple flavoring; stir into the oat mixture and mix well. Press half of this mixture onto bottom of buttered 9" x 13" pan. Spread filling evenly on top of crust. Roll out remaining dough between two sheets of wax paper to 9" x 13". Place top crust over fruit mixture, and press lightly. Bake at 325° for 25-30 minutes. If a light golden brown top crust is desired, briefly place under broiler. Remove from oven and allow bars to cool completely before serving. **Yield: 36 bars**

Per Bar: **Calories:** 105.3 **Carbs:** 18.3g **Fiber:** 2.3g
Fat: 3.5g **Sodium:** 1.2mg **Net Carbs:** 14.9g

Vanilla Sandwich Cookies

6 tablespoons unsalted butter, softened
1 cup xylitol
¼ cup unsweetened applesauce
1 egg
1 tablespoon vanilla extract
1 teaspoon maple flavoring
2 cups spelt flour or whole wheat pastry flour
½ cup arrowroot powder
½ teaspoon baking soda
⅜ teaspoon salt
Additional xylitol for rolling cookies

Cream butter and xylitol; gradually add applesauce during creaming process. Beat in egg, vanilla extract, and maple flavoring, and set aside. In another bowl combine flour, arrowroot powder, baking soda and salt; gradually stir into creamed mixture. Refrigerate for 1 hour or until dough can be handled easily. Shape dough into balls using ½ tablespoon of dough per cookie and roll in xylitol. Place on parchment lined cookie sheet, and flatten slightly with bottom of glass dipped in xylitol. Bake at 350° for 8-10 minutes or until cookies are golden brown. Allow cookies to cool completely before putting together in pairs with one of the fillings listed on pages 69–72.
Yield: 27 sandwich cookies

Per Sandwich Cookie Without Filling: **Calories:** 80 **Carbs:** 14.2g **Fiber:** 1g **Fat:** 3g **Sodium:** 58.7mg **Net Carbs:** 7g

Fillings For Sandwich Cookies

Cherry Filling

6 tablespoons unsalted butter, softened
2 cups powdered xylitol, sifted
⅔ cup dry milk powder
2½ tablespoons water
1½ teaspoons cherry flavoring

Whip butter until light; gradually beat in xylitol and dry milk powder, adding water as needed until mixture is smooth and correct consistency. Stir in cherry flavoring. **Yield: 1¼ cups filling**

Per Tablespoon: **Calories:** 62.5 **Carbs:** 21g **Fiber:** 0g
Fat: 3.5g **Sodium:** 13mg **Net Carbs:** 11.1g

Chocolate Filling

4 tablespoons unsalted butter, softened
2 cups powdered xylitol, sifted
2 ounces unsweetened chocolate bar, melted
1 teaspoon vanilla extract
2 tablespoons fat-free milk

Whip butter until light; gradually beat in xylitol. Add melted chocolate a small amount at a time while beating constantly, adding vanilla extract and milk until mixture is smooth and correct consistency. **Yield: 1½ cups filling**

Per Tablespoon: **Calories:** 50.2 **Carbs:** 17.3g **Fiber:** 0.4g
Fat: 3.2g **Sodium:** 1.1mg **Net Carbs:** 8.7g

Fillings For Sandwich Cookies

Crème De Menthe Filling

4½ tablespoons unsalted butter, softened
2¼ cups powdered xylitol, sifted
3 tablespoons dry milk powder
2 tablespoons crème de menthe liqueur

Whip butter until light; gradually beat in xylitol and dry milk powder, adding crème de menthe and water as needed until mixture is smooth and correct consistency. **Yield: 1⅛ cups filling**

Per Tablespoon: **Calories:** 64.8 **Carbs:** 26g
Fiber: 0g **Fat:** 2.9g **Sodium:** 4.4mg **Net Carbs:** 13.6g

Lemon Filling

6 tablespoons unsalted butter, softened
2 cups powdered xylitol, sifted
⅔ cup dry milk powder
4 tablespoons freshly squeezed lemon juice
2 teaspoons finely grated lemon zest

Whip butter until light; gradually beat in xylitol and dry milk powder, adding lemon juice as needed until mixture is smooth and correct consistency. Stir in lemon zest. **Yield: 1¼ cups filling**

Per Tablespoon: **Calories:** 63.3 **Carbs:** 21.3g **Fiber:** 0g
Fat: 3.5g **Sodium:** 12.9mg **Net Carbs:** 11.4g

Orange Filling

Follow above directions for Lemon Filling, except substitute fresh orange juice for lemon juice and orange zest for lemon zest.

Per Tablespoon: **Calories:** 62.7 **Carbs:** 21.1g
Fiber: 0g **Fat:** 3.5g **Sodium:** 12.9mg **Net Carbs:** 11.1g

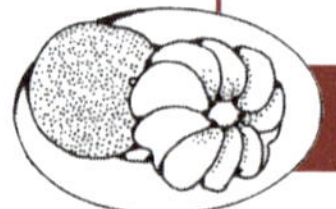

Fillings For Sandwich Cookies

Peppermint Filling

4½ tablespoons unsalted butter, softened
2¼ cups powdered xylitol, sifted
3 tablespoons dry milk powder
¼ teaspoon peppermint extract
2 tablespoons water

Whip butter until light; gradually beat in xylitol and dry milk powder, adding peppermint extract and water as needed until mixture is smooth and correct consistency. **Yield: 1 1/3 cups filling**

Per Tablespoon: **Calories:** 49.5 **Carbs:** 21.6g **Fiber:** 0g
Fat: 2.5g **Sodium:** 3.7mg **Net Carbs:** 11g

Vanilla Filling

4½ tablespoons unsalted butter, softened
2¼ cups powdered xylitol, sifted
3 tablespoons dry milk powder
1½ teaspoons vanilla extract
1½ tablespoons water

Whip butter until light; gradually beat in xylitol and dry milk powder, adding vanilla extract and water as needed until mixture is smooth and correct consistency. **Yield: 1 1/3 cups filling**

Per Tablespoon: **Calories:** 69.5 **Carbs:** 29.8g **Fiber:** 0g
Fat: 3.4g **Sodium:** 5.1mg **Net Carbs:** 15.2g

Fillings For Sandwich Cookies

Peanut Butter Filling

5 tablespoons unsalted butter, softened
6 tablespoons smooth peanut butter
1⅓ cups powdered xylitol, sifted
6 tablespoons dry milk powder
½ teaspoon vanilla extract
2 teaspoons water

Whip butter and peanut butter together until light. Gradually beat in powdered xylitol and milk powder, adding vanilla extract and water until filling is desired spreading consistency. **Yield: 1 1/8 cups filling**

Per Tablespoon: **Calories:** 82.8 **Carbs:** 16.5g **Fiber:** 0.3g **Fat:** 5.9g **Sodium:** 32.7mg **Net Carbs:** 8.8g

Breads & Muffins

Banana Nut Bread

4 tablespoons unsalted butter, softened
⅔ cup xylitol
2 tablespoons unsweetened applesauce
2 eggs
1 teaspoon vanilla extract
½ cup oat flour
1¼ cups spelt flour or whole wheat pastry flour
½ teaspoon salt
2½ teaspoons baking powder
1 teaspoon baking soda
1 cup mashed bananas
½ cup chopped pecans, lightly toasted

Cream butter and xylitol; gradually add applesauce during creaming process. Add eggs and vanilla extract, and beat well. Combine flours, salt, baking powder, and baking soda, and stir into creamed mixture alternately with mashed bananas. Fold in the nuts, and pour into a buttered and floured 9" x 5" x 3" loaf pan. Bake at 350° for 40-45 minutes or until toothpick inserted in center comes out clean. Cover with aluminum foil to prevent over-browning, if necessary. **Yield: 16 servings.**

Per Serving: **Calories**: 118.6 **Carbs**: 15.8g **Fiber:** 1.6g
Fat: 6.5g **Sodium**: 217.3mg **Net Carbs**: 7.2g

Blueberry Lemon Pecan Scones

1½ cups plus 2 tablespoons spelt flour
or whole wheat pastry flour
⅓ cup xylitol
1½ teaspoons baking powder
¾ teaspoon baking soda
½ teaspoon salt
4 tablespoons unsalted butter
¼ cup finely chopped pecans
1½ teaspoons finely grated lemon zest
⅔ cup blueberries, frozen
1 egg, beaten
1 tablespoon unsweetened applesauce
½ cup reduced fat sour cream
Optional:
Egg wash (1 egg beaten with 1 tablespoon water)
1 tablespoon xylitol

Thoroughly combine flour, xylitol, baking powder, baking soda, and salt. Cut in butter until mixture resembles fine crumbs. Stir in pecans, lemon zest, and blueberries. In a separate bowl, combine egg, applesauce, and sour cream, and stir into flour mixture just until dry ingredients are moistened.

Line a baking sheet with parchment paper, and lightly oil the top of the paper. Transfer the dough to the paper. Lightly flour hands and shape the dough into a 7" diameter round. Using a sharp knife that has been floured, cut the round into 8 wedges. If desired, brush top of scones with egg wash, and sprinkle with xylitol before baking.

Bake scones at 350° for 25 minutes or until lightly browned. These scones are best when served immediately after baking.
Yield: 8 scones

Per Scone:	**Calories:** 215.1	**Carbs:** 26g	**Fiber:** 3.1g
Fat: 11.6g	**Sodium:** 351.6mg	**Net Carbs:** 16g	

Cinnamon Raisin Scones

Follow directions for Blueberry Lemon Pecan Scones, page 75, with the following changes:

1. Add ¾ teaspoon cinnamon to dry ingredients before adding butter.
2. Delete the pecans and lemon zest.
3. Delete the blueberries, and add ½ cup chopped rehydrated raisins.
4. If desired, brush top of scones with milk and sprinkle with 2 tablespoons xylitol combined with ½ teaspoon cinnamon before baking.

Per Scone: **Calories:** 212.2 **Carbs:** 31.1g **Fiber:** 2.9g
Fat: 9.2g **Sodium:** 352.6mg **Net Carbs:** 21.2g

Blueberry Muffins

2 cups spelt flour or whole wheat pastry flour
1 cup xylitol
2½ teaspoons baking powder
1 teaspoon baking soda
¼ teaspoon salt
1½ teaspoons finely grated lemon zest
1 cup fresh or frozen blueberries
2 eggs
1 cup plain low-fat yogurt
2 tablespoons extra virgin olive oil
1½ tablespoons unsweetened applesauce

In medium bowl combine flour, xylitol, baking powder, baking soda, salt, and lemon zest. Gently stir blueberries into flour mixture until berries are coated with flour. In another bowl mix eggs, yogurt, olive oil, and applesauce. Add liquid mixture to dry ingredients all at once, and stir just until flour is moistened. Coat inside of muffin cups with nonstick spray. Spoon batter into muffin pan and bake at 375° for 20 minutes or until muffins are light golden and toothpick inserted in center comes out clean. **Yield: 14 muffins**

Per Muffin: **Calories**: 129.9 **Carbs**: 25.7g **Fiber**: 2.1g
Fat: 3.4g **Sodium**: 218.7mg **Net Carbs**: 11.7g

Carrot Spice Muffins

1 cup spelt flour or whole wheat pastry flour
½ cup quick-cooking oats, uncooked
1 teaspoon baking soda
2 teaspoons baking powder
½ teaspoon cinnamon
¼ teaspoon nutmeg
⅛ teaspoon ginger
⅛ teaspoon allspice
½ cup xylitol
1 egg
½ cup reduced-fat sour cream
2 tablespoons extra virgin olive oil
1 tablespoon unsweetened applesauce
½ teaspoon vanilla extract
1½ cups finely grated carrots
½ cup raisins, rehydrated (optional)

Combine flour, oats, baking soda, baking powder, spices, and xylitol in a large bowl. In another bowl mix together remaining ingredients. Add liquid ingredients all at once to flour mixture, and stir just until flour is moistened. Coat inside of muffin cups with nonstick spray. Spoon batter into muffin pan and bake at 350° for 18-20 minutes or until toothpick inserted in center comes out clean. **Yield: 12 muffins**

Per Muffin: **Calories**: 114.1 **Carbs**: 18g **Fiber**: 1.8g
Fat: 4.6g **Sodium**: 188.1mg **Net Carbs**: 9.2g

Chocolate Chip Orange Muffins

1½ cups spelt flour or whole wheat pastry flour
½ cup plus 2 tablespoons xylitol
2 teaspoons baking powder
½ teaspoon salt
2 ½ ounces xylitol-sweetened dark chocolate bars, chopped
2 tablespoons freshly grated orange zest
1 egg
½ cup reduced-fat sour cream
2 tablespoons unsweetened applesauce
2 tablespoons extra virgin olive oil

Combine flour, xylitol, baking powder, salt, chocolate, and orange zest in a medium size bowl. In another bowl mix together remaining ingredients. Add the liquid ingredients all at once to the flour mixture, and stir just until flour is moistened. Coat inside of muffin cups with non-stick spray. Spoon batter into muffin pan and bake at 350° for 15-20 minutes or until toothpick inserted in center comes out clean.
Yield: 12 muffins

Per Muffin: **Calories:** 146.8 **Carbs:** 23.2g **Fiber:** 2.3g
Fat: 7.4g **Sodium:** 175mg **Net Carbs:** 10.5g

Cinnamon Apple Muffins

1¾ cups spelt flour or whole wheat pastry flour
3 teaspoons baking powder
1½ teaspoons baking soda
½ teaspoon salt
2 teaspoons cinnamon
1 cup xylitol
1 tablespoon lecithin granules
2 tablespoons unsalted butter, melted
2 eggs, beaten
⅔ cup reduced-fat sour cream
2 tablespoons unsweetened applesauce
1 cup finely chopped apples (not necessary to peel)

In large bowl combine flour, baking powder, baking soda, salt, cinnamon, xylitol, and lecithin granules; mix well. In another bowl mix together butter, egg, sour cream and applesauce. Add liquid ingredients to flour mixture and stir just until dry ingredients are moistened; stir in apples. Coat inside of muffin cups with non-stick spray. Spoon batter into muffin pan. Bake in a 375° oven for 18 minutes or until toothpick inserted in center comes out clean. **Yield: 12 muffins**

Per Muffin: **Calories:** 154.5 **Carbs:** 28.2g **Fiber:** 2.2g
Fat: 5.3g **Sodium:** 366.5mg **Net Carbs:** 12g

Maple Pecan Sour Cream Muffins

4 tablespoons unsalted butter, softened
1 cup xylitol
1½ teaspoons maple flavoring
2 eggs
1¼ cups spelt flour or whole wheat pastry flour
2½ teaspoons baking powder
1 teaspoon baking soda
¼ teaspoon salt
¾ cup reduced-fat sour cream
⅔ cup coarsely chopped pecans, lightly toasted

Cream butter and xylitol, then add maple flavoring; beat in eggs one at a time just until incorporated. In another bowl, combine flour, baking powder, baking soda, and salt. Gradually add the dry ingredients to the creamed mixture alternately with the sour cream, mixing only until batter is smooth. Fold in pecans. Coat inside of muffin cups with non-stick spray. Spoon batter into muffin pan, and bake at 375° for 15-20 minutes, or until toothpick inserted in center comes out clean. **Yield: 12 muffins.**

Per Muffin: **Calories:** 189.9 **Carbs:** 24g **Fiber:** 1.8g
Fat: 11.5g **Sodium:** 251.7mg **Net Carbs:** 8.2g

Oatmeal Muffins

1 cup rolled oats, uncooked
¾ cup reduced-fat sour cream
¼ cup water
1 egg
2 tablespoons extra virgin olive oil
4½ tablespoons unsweetened applesauce
½ cup raisins, rehydrated (optional)
1 cup xylitol
1½ cups spelt flour or whole wheat pastry flour
2 teaspoons baking powder
1 teaspoon baking soda
½ teaspoon salt
½ teaspoon cinnamon
¼ teaspoon cloves
¼ teaspoon mace
1 teaspoon finely grated lemon zest

Combine oats, sour cream, and water in a large bowl; cover, and let stand at room temperature for 1-2 hours. Stir in egg, olive oil, and applesauce; mix well. Stir in drained raisins, if desired. In another bowl combine remaining ingredients, and add all at once to sour cream mixture, stirring just until flour is moistened. Coat inside of muffin cups with non-stick spray. Spoon batter into muffin pan and bake at 350° for 20-22 minutes or until toothpick inserted in center comes out clean. **Yield: 14 muffins**

Per Muffin: **Calories:** 141.4 **Carbs:** 25.7g **Fiber:** 2g
Fat: 4.8g **Sodium:** 239.5mg **Net Carbs:** 11.7g

Orange Pecan Tea Bread

1⅔ cups spelt flour or whole wheat pastry flour
¾ cup xylitol
2½ teaspoons baking powder
1 teaspoon baking soda
½ teaspoon salt
2–3 tablespoons freshly grated orange zest
⅓ cup finely chopped pecans
1 egg
2½ tablespoons extra virgin olive oil
1 tablespoon unsweetened applesauce
⅔ cup freshly squeezed orange juice
⅓ cup reduced-fat sour cream

Combine flour, xylitol, baking powder, baking soda, salt, orange zest, and pecans in large bowl. In another bowl combine remaining ingredients, and mix well. Add egg mixture to dry ingredients, and stir just until flour is moistened. Spoon into 3 buttered and floured 5" x 3" x 2" miniature loaf pans, and bake at 350° for 30 minutes or until toothpick inserted in center comes out clean. **Yield: 3 loaves, 6 servings/loaf**

Per Serving: **Calories:** 97.1 **Carbs:** 15g **Fiber:** 1.4g
Fat: 4.5g **Sodium:** 192.1mg **Net Carbs:** 6.6g

Peanut Butter Muffins

1½ cups spelt flour or whole wheat pastry flour
2 teaspoons baking powder
1 teaspoon baking soda
¼ teaspoon salt (increase to ½ teaspoon if using salt-free peanut butter)
1 cup xylitol
½ cup unsweetened applesauce
½ cup smooth peanut butter
¾ cup reduced-fat sour cream
1 teaspoon vanilla extract

Combine flour, baking powder, baking soda, salt, and xylitol in a large bowl. In another bowl, combine remaining ingredients. Add peanut butter mixture all at once to dry ingredients, and stir just until flour is moistened. Coat inside of muffin cups with non-stick spray. Spoon batter into muffin pan, and bake at 350° for 20 minutes or until toothpick inserted in center comes out clean. **Yield: 14 muffins**

Per Muffin: **Calories:** 153 **Carbs:** 24g **Fiber:** 1.9g
Fat: 6.8g **Sodium:** 234.9mg **Net Carbs:** 10g

Note: These can also be frosted with Peanut Butter Cream Cheese Frosting, p. 93 and served as cupcakes.

Variation: Peanut Butter and Chocolate Chip Muffins—Follow directions for Peanut Butter Muffins, and stir 3 ounces of maltitol-sweetened dark chocolate (chopped) into dry ingredients before adding peanut butter mixture.

Per Muffin: **Calories:** 180.1 **Carbs:** 27.4g **Fiber:** 2.3g
Fat: 8.9g **Sodium:** 241.1mg **Net Carbs:** 10g

Pumpkin Bread

Batter:
2 eggs
¼ cup extra virgin olive oil
2 tablespoons unsweetened applesauce
1 cup canned pumpkin
½ teaspoon vanilla extract
1⅔ cups spelt flour or whole wheat pastry flour
1⅓ cups xylitol
1½ teaspoons baking powder
½ teaspoon salt
1½ teaspoons cinnamon
½ teaspoon nutmeg
¼ teaspoon ginger
⅛ teaspoon cloves
½ cup chopped pecans

Topping:
2½ tablespoons xylitol
¼ teaspoon cinnamon

Combine eggs, olive oil, applesauce, pumpkin, and vanilla extract in large bowl; mix well. In another bowl, combine all remaining ingredients. Stir dry ingredients into pumpkin mixture; spoon into three buttered and floured 5" x 3" x 2" miniature loaf pans. Stir xylitol and cinnamon together for topping, and sprinkle over each loaf before baking. Bake at 350° for 50-60 minutes or until toothpick inserted in center comes out clean. Cover loaves with aluminum foil during latter part of baking to prevent over browning, if necessary.

Yield: 3 loaves, 6 servings/loaf

Per Serving: **Calories:** 133.8 **Carbs:** 23.3g **Fiber:** 2g
Fat: 6.1g **Sodium:** 137.3mg **Net Carbs:** 7.1g

Pumpkin Streusel Muffins

Muffins:

1 egg
3 tablespoons plain low-fat yogurt
1 tablespoon water
¾ cup canned pumpkin
2 tablespoons extra virgin olive oil
1 teaspoon vanilla extract
1¾ cups spelt flour or whole wheat pastry flour
½ cup plus 2 tablespoons xylitol
½ teaspoon salt
½ teaspoon nutmeg
2½ teaspoons baking powder
1 teaspoon baking soda
1 teaspoon cinnamon
2 teaspoons lecithin granules

Streusel Topping:

¼ cup xylitol
½ teaspoon cinnamon
1 tablespoon unsalted butter
¼ cup finely chopped pecans
3 tablespoons quick-cooking oats, uncooked

In medium bowl, combine egg, yogurt, water, pumpkin, olive oil, and vanilla extract; mix well. In another bowl, stir together flour, xylitol, salt, nutmeg, baking powder, baking soda, cinnamon, and lecithin. Add pumpkin mixture to dry ingredients and stir just until flour is moistened. Coat inside of muffin cups with non-stick spray. Spoon batter into muffin pan. Combine ingredients for the streusel topping, and sprinkle evenly over each muffin. Bake at 350° for 18-20 minutes or until lightly browned. **Yield: 12 muffins**

Per Muffin: **Calories:** 153.5 **Carbs:** 26.4g **Fiber:** 2.7g
Fat: 6.1g **Sodium:** 323.2mg **Net Carbs:** 11.5g

Frostings, Fillings, and Toppings

Chocolate Buttercream Frosting

6 tablespoons unsalted butter, softened
2 cups powdered xylitol, sifted
½ cup unsweetened cocoa powder, sifted
2-3 tablespoons fat-free milk
1 teaspoon vanilla extract

Beat butter until creamy. Combine powdered xylitol and cocoa powder and gradually beat into butter alternately with milk until frosting reaches the desired consistency for spreading. Stir in vanilla extract. **Yield: 2 cups frosting**

Per Tablespoon: **Calories:** 38 **Carbs:** 13.2g **Fiber:** 0.4g
Fat: 2.3g **Sodium:** 1.3mg **Net Carbs:** 6.6g

Chocolate Ganache

3 ounces unsweetened chocolate bar
½ cup whipping cream
¾ cup xylitol
¾ cup reduced-fat sour cream

Melt chocolate in top of double boiler over hot water. Stir in whipping cream, and gradually add xylitol, stirring until it is completely dissolved. Remove from heat, and stir in sour cream until thoroughly blended. **Yield: 1½ cups**

Note: This version of chocolate ganache contains much less fat than the traditional recipe. Chocolate Ganache is very versatile. When warm, it may be poured over cake and served as a glaze. As the ganache cools, it becomes more firm, and may be used as a filling between cake layers. The cooled ganache may also be whipped and used as a rich and creamy frosting.

Per Tablespoon: **Calories:** 61 **Carbs:** 7g **Fiber:** 0.6g
Fat: 4.7g **Sodium:** 8mg **Net Carbs:** 1.1g

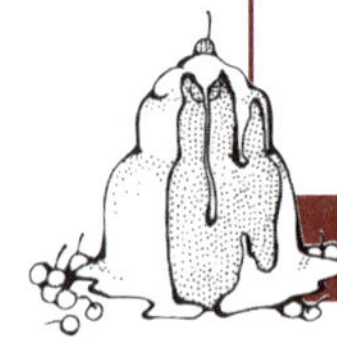

Chocolate Sauce

3 ounces unsweetened chocolate bar
¾ cup water
1½ tablespoons unsalted butter
1 cup xylitol
1½ teaspoons vanilla extract

In double boiler, melt chocolate in water; add butter and stir until melted. Add xylitol and stir until it has completely dissolved. Transfer to direct heat and bring chocolate mixture to a low boil. Let boil for 3-5 minutes, stirring frequently. Remove from heat and stir in vanilla extract.
Yield: 1 1/8 cups sauce

Note: This sauce is thin when warm, but thickens as it cools in the refrigerator. Delicious when spooned over ice cream or cake.

Per Tablespoon: **Calories:** 55.9 **Carbs:** 10.6g **Fiber:** 0.7g
Fat: 3.5g **Sodium:** 1mg **Net Carbs:** 0.6g

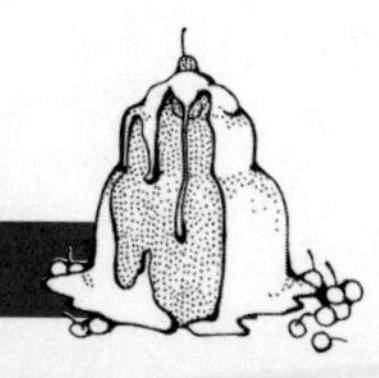

Coconut-Pecan Frosting

5 tablespoons unsalted butter
5 tablespoons unsweetened applesauce
¾ cup xylitol
4 egg yolks
4 teaspoons lecithin granules
4 tablespoons dry milk powder
½ cup water
¼ teaspoon maple flavoring
1¼ teaspoons vanilla extract
1 cup shredded unsweetened coconut
⅔ cup chopped pecans

Melt butter in heavy saucepan. In small bowl, combine applesauce, xylitol, egg yolks, lecithin granules, and milk powder; stir into melted butter. Slowly stir in water. Cook over medium heat, stirring constantly, for 10 minutes. Stir in maple flavoring, vanilla extract, coconut, and pecans. Allow to cool before spreading on cake. **Yield: 2 cups frosting**

Per Tablespoon: **Calories:** 69.6 **Carbs:** 5.5g **Fiber:** 0.7g
Fat: 5.8g **Sodium:** 5.3mg **Net Carbs:** 0.9g

Crème De Menthe Cream Cheese Frosting

4 tablespoons unsalted butter, softened
8 ounces reduced-fat cream cheese, softened
¼ cup xylitol
1½ tablespoons crème de menthe liqueur

Beat butter and cream cheese until light and fluffy. Gradually beat in xylitol; stir in crème de menthe. Frosts one 9" x 13" cake. **Yield: 1⅞ cups frosting**

Per Tablespoon: **Calories:** 39.7 **Carbs:** 2g **Fiber:** 0g
Fat: 3.3g **Sodium:** 30.4mg **Net Carbs:** 0.6g

Lemon Cream Cheese Frosting

4 tablespoons unsalted butter, softened
8 ounces reduced-fat cream cheese, softened
½ cup plus 2 tablespoons xylitol
1 tablespoon freshly squeezed lemon juice
1 tablespoon grated lemon zest

Beat butter and cream cheese until light and fluffy. Gradually beat in xylitol; stir in lemon juice and lemon zest. **Yield: 2¼ cups frosting**

Per Tablespoon: **Calories:** 34.9 **Carbs:** 3.2g **Fiber:** 0g
Fat: 2.8g **Sodium:** 25.3mg **Net Carbs:** 0.2g

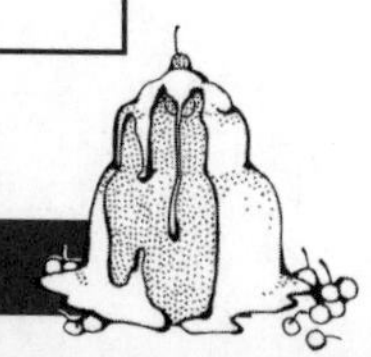

Maple Butter Pecan Frosting

4½ tablespoons unsalted butter, softened
3 cups powdered xylitol, sifted
2½ tablespoons fat-free milk
1½ teaspoons maple flavoring
⅓ cup finely chopped pecans, toasted

Beat butter until creamy; gradually beat in powdered xylitol alternately with milk and maple flavoring until frosting reaches the desired consistency for spreading. Stir in toasted pecans. **Yield: 1⅞ cups frosting**

Per Tablespoon: **Calories:** 47.9 **Carbs:** 20.1g **Fiber:** 0.1g **Fat:** 2.6g **Sodium:** 0.9mg **Net Carbs:** 10g

Mocha Cream Cheese Frosting

4 tablespoons unsalted butter, softened
8 ounces reduced-fat cream cheese, softened
½ cup plus 2 tablespoons xylitol
3 tablespoons unsweetened cocoa powder, sifted
1¼ teaspoons vanilla extract
1 teaspoon coffee extract
½ teaspoon freshly squeezed lemon juice

Beat butter and cream cheese until light and fluffy. Combine xylitol and cocoa powder; gradually beat into cream cheese mixture. Stir in vanilla extract, coffee extract, and lemon juice. **Yield: 2 cups plus 3 tablespoons frosting**

Per Tablespoon: **Calories:** 40.5 **Carbs:** 3.8g **Fiber:** 0.2g **Fat:** 3.2g **Sodium:** 28.4mg **Net Carbs:** 0.3g

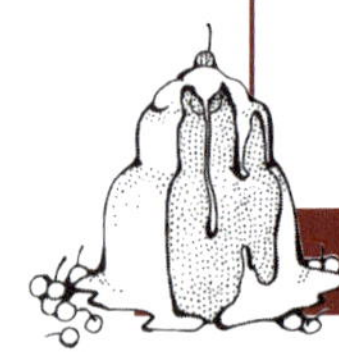

Peanut Butter Cream Cheese Frosting

4 tablespoons unsalted butter, softened
8 ounces reduced-fat cream cheese, softened
½ cup smooth peanut butter
2 cups powdered xylitol, sifted
1 tablespoon fat-free milk
½ teaspoon vanilla extract

Beat butter and cream cheese until light and fluffy. Add peanut butter and beat until well blended. Gradually add powdered xylitol and beat until frosting is smooth. Stir in milk and vanilla extract until frosting reaches the desired consistency for spreading. **Yield: 2½ cups frosting**

Per Tablespoon: **Calories:** 56.2 **Carbs:** 10.8g **Fiber:** 0.2g
Fat: 4.1g **Sodium:** 37.8mg **Net Carbs:** 5.6g

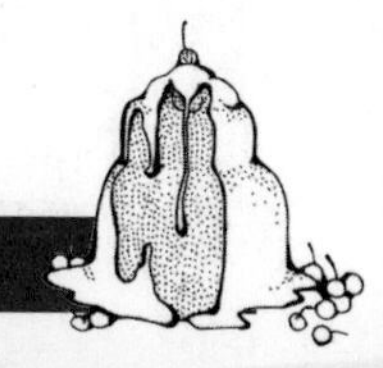

Seven Minute Frosting

2 egg whites
1 cup xylitol
¼ teaspoon cream of tartar
¼ cup water
1 teaspoon vanilla extract

Combine egg whites, xylitol, cream of tartar, and water in top of double boiler. Beat at high speed for 1 minute. Bring water in bottom of double boiler to rapid boil; beat for another 7 minutes or until peaks form when beater is raised. Remove from boiling water, and transfer frosting to large bowl. Add vanilla extract, and beat until frosting reaches spreading consistency. Generously fills and frosts two 8" or 9" cake layers or a 9" x 13" cake. **Yield: 2½ cups frosting**

Note: If desired, cherry flavoring may be substituted for the vanilla extract.

Per Tablespoon: **Calories:** 11.3 **Carbs:** 4.2g **Fiber:** 0g
Fat: 0g **Sodium:** 2.8mg **Net Carbs:** 0g

Vanilla Cream Cheese Frosting

4 tablespoons unsalted butter, softened
8 ounces reduced-fat cream cheese, softened
½ cup plus 2 tablespoons xylitol
1½ teaspoons vanilla extract

Beat butter and cream cheese until light and fluffy. Gradually beat in xylitol; stir in vanilla extract. Frosts one 9" x 13" cake. **Yield: 2¼ cups frosting**

Per Tablespoon: **Calories:** 35.2 **Carbs:** 3.1g **Fiber:** 0g
Fat: 2.8g **Sodium:** 25.4mg **Net Carbs:** 0.2g

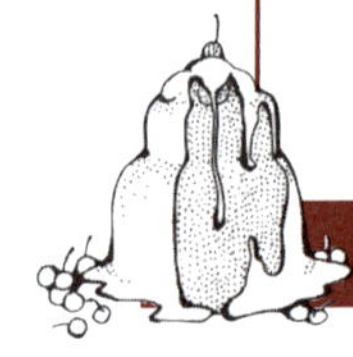

Vanilla Cream Custard Filling

- 1½ cups fat-free milk
- ⅔ cup xylitol
- 2 tablespoons arrowroot powder
- ¼ teaspoon salt
- 3 egg yolks
- 1 teaspoon vanilla extract
- ¼ cup reduced-fat sour cream
- ¼ cup whipping cream

Place milk in a small saucepan, and heat to almost boiling. Remove from heat and set aside. Combine xylitol, arrowroot powder, and salt in a medium bowl. Add egg yolks and beat until thoroughly incorporated. Slowly add scalded milk to egg mixture, and stir until well blended. Transfer to top of double boiler; heat water in bottom of double boiler to boiling, stirring mixture constantly until thick and smooth. Stir in vanilla extract and sour cream. Pour custard into a medium bowl and refrigerate until cooled. Beat whipping cream until soft peaks form; gently fold into chilled custard filling.
Yield: 2¼ cups filling

Per Tablespoon: **Calories:** 26.1 **Carbs:** 4.2g **Fiber:** 0g
Fat: 1.2g **Sodium:** 22.9mg **Net Carbs:** 1.1g

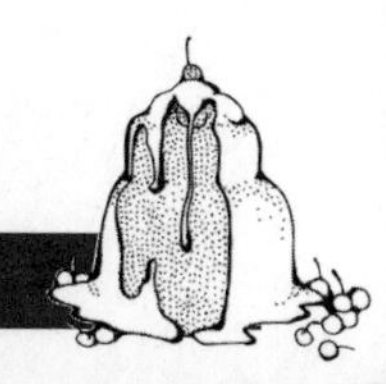

Ice Creams, Drinks, Etc.

French Vanilla Ice Cream

2 cups fat-free milk
¼ cup arrowroot powder
1⅓ cups xylitol
4 egg yolks
2½ teaspoons vanilla extract
1 cup reduced-fat sour cream
1 cup whipping cream

Place milk in a small saucepan and heat to almost boiling. Remove from heat and set aside. Combine arrowroot powder and xylitol in a medium bowl. Thoroughly beat egg yolks into xylitol mixture. Slowly add scalded milk to egg mixture, stirring until well blended. Transfer this mixture to top of double boiler, and cook over boiling water, stirring constantly, until custard is thick and smooth. Strain, if necessary. Stir in vanilla extract, and pour mixture into a large bowl. Stir in sour cream until thoroughly combined, cover bowl, and refrigerate until chilled.

Beat whipping cream until soft peaks form. Gently fold whipped cream into chilled custard mixture. Transfer to small automatic ice cream maker and freeze. **Yield: 1½ quarts or twelve ½ cup servings**

Per Serving: **Calories:** 194.1 **Carbs:** 25.3g **Fiber:** 0.1g
Fat: 11.7g **Sodium:** 45.8mg **Net Carbs:** 6.5

Blueberry Ice Cream

Follow above directions for French Vanilla Ice Cream with the following additions: combine 1 cup pureed blueberries, 2 tablespoons freshly squeezed lemon juice, and ½ teaspoon almond extract. Stir into custard after sour cream is added and continue process as above. **Yield: fourteen ½ cup servings**

Per Serving: **Calories:** 176.7 **Carbs:** 24.3g **Fiber:** 0.5g
Fat: 10.1g **Sodium:** 39.5mg **Net Carbs:** 7.9g

Butter Pecan Ice Cream

Follow directions for French Vanilla Ice Cream, and add 1 teaspoon butter flavoring along with the vanilla extract. After ice cream is removed from ice cream maker, stir in 2/3 cup chopped pecans that have been lightly toasted.
Yield: thirteen ½ cup servings

Per Serving: **Calories:** 217.8 **Carbs:** 24.1g **Fiber:** 0.6g
Fat: 14.9g **Sodium:** 42.3mg **Net Carbs:** 6.3g

Chocolate Chip Mint Ice Cream

Follow directions for French Vanilla Ice Cream, and add 1 teaspoon peppermint extract along with the vanilla extract. After ice cream is removed from ice cream maker, stir in 2 ounces of finely chopped xylitol-sweetened chocolate bar.
Yield: twelve ½ cup servings

Per Serving: **Calories:** 215.2 **Carbs:** 28g **Fiber:** 0.6g
Fat: 13.9g **Sodium:** 46.3mg **Net Carbs:** 7.4g

Rich Chocolate Ice Cream

Follow directions for French Vanilla Ice Cream, except add 2 ounces unsweetened chocolate bar to custard along with the vanilla extract and stir until chocolate is melted. Continue to follow directions for French Vanilla Ice Cream.
Yield: twelve ½ cup servings

Per Serving: **Calories:** 218.7 **Carbs:** 26.6g **Fiber:** 0.8g
Fat: 14.4g **Sodium:** 46.5mg **Net Carbs:** 7.1g

Dark Chocolate Ice Cream

Follow directions for French Vanilla Ice Cream, except increase xylitol to 1¾ cup and add 4 ounces unsweetened chocolate bar to custard along with the vanilla extract and stir until chocolate is melted. Continue to follow directions for French Vanilla Ice Cream. **Yield: thirteen ½ cup servings**

Per Serving: **Calories:** 237.6 **Carbs:** 31.1g **Fiber:** 1.4g
Fat: 15.7g **Sodium:** 43.5mg **Net Carbs:** 7.1g

Dark Chocolate Mint Ice Cream

Follow above directions for Dark Chocolate Ice Cream and add 1 teaspoon peppermint extract along with the vanilla extract. **Yield: thirteen ½ cup servings**

Per Serving: **Calories:** 237.6 **Carbs:** 31.1g **Fiber:** 1.4g
Fat: 15.7g **Sodium:** 43.5mg **Net Carbs:** 7.1g

Coffee Ice Cream

In the recipe for French Vanilla Ice Cream, make the following changes: In saucepan, bring 1/3 cup water to a boil, and stir in 2 tablespoons instant coffee granules until completely dissolved. Add 1 2/3 cup milk to the hot coffee and heat to almost boiling. Remove from heat and set aside. Continue to follow directions for French Vanilla Ice Cream. **Yield: twelve ½ cup servings**

Per Serving: **Calories: 192.7** **Carbs:** 25.1g **Fiber: 0.1g**
Fat: 11.7g **Sodium:** 42.5mg **Net Carbs:** 6.4g

Peach Ice Cream

1 cup xylitol
1 tablespoon arrowroot powder
1 cup whole milk
2 cups pureed peaches
2 tablespoons freshly squeezed lemon juice
1 cup whipping cream

Combine xylitol and arrowroot powder, gradually stir in milk, and cook until thick, stirring constantly. Transfer mixture to a large bowl, cover, and refrigerate until cold. Stir in peach puree and lemon juice, and refrigerate until mixture is well chilled. Beat whipping cream until soft peaks form. Gently fold whipped cream into peach mixture; transfer to small automatic ice cream maker and freeze. **Yield: 1½ quarts or twelve ½ cup servings**

Per Serving: **Calories:** 131.9 **Carbs:** 19.9g **Fiber:** 0.6g
Fat: 8.1g **Sodium:** 15.7mg **Net Carbs:** 5.3g

Strawberry Ice Cream

¾ cup xylitol, divided
1 tablespoon arrowroot powder
1 cup whole milk
2 cups pureed strawberries
½ teaspoon vanilla extract
1 cup whipping cream

Combine ½ cup xylitol with arrowroot powder, gradually stir in milk, and cook until thick, stirring constantly. Transfer mixture to a large bowl, cover, and refrigerate until cold. In another bowl, stir pureed strawberries and remaining ¼ cup xylitol together until xylitol dissolves; refrigerate until well chilled. Stir strawberry mixture and vanilla extract into milk mixture. Beat whipping cream until soft peaks form. Gently fold whipped cream into strawberry mixture; transfer to small automatic ice cream maker and freeze. **Yield: 1½ quarts or twelve ½ cup servings**

Per Serving: **Calories:** 121.1 **Carbs:** 15.5g **Fiber:** 0.8g
Fat: 8.1g **Sodium:** 16.1mg **Net Carbs:** 4.3g

Iced Tea

8 cups cold water
8 regular size (or 2 family size) decaffeinated tea bags
1½ cups xylitol

Bring 8 cups cold water to a boil. Remove from heat, add tea bags, and cover. Allow tea to steep for 5-10 minutes, and remove tea bags. Add xylitol, and stir until completely dissolved. Stir in 7 cups cold water and refrigerate. Pour into ice-filled glasses, and serve with lemon or orange slices. Very refreshing! **Yield: approximately 1 gallon iced tea or sixteen 8 ounce servings**

Per Serving: **Calories:** 37.7 **Carbs:** 15.7g **Fiber:** 0g
Fat: 0g **Sodium:** 2.4mg **Net Carbs:** 0g

Lemonade

1½ cups freshly squeezed lemon juice
6 cups cold water
1 cup plus 2 tablespoons xylitol

Combine lemon juice and cold water. Stir in xylitol until dissolved. Pour into ice-filled glasses. **Yield: 2 quarts or eight 8 ounce servings**

Per Serving: **Calories:** 68 **Carbs:** 27.5g **Fiber:** 0.2g
Fat: 0g **Sodium:** 4mg **Net Carbs:** 3.8g

Prune Puree

½ cup pitted prunes
1 cup water

In blender, combine prunes and water. Process on high for several minutes, or until mixture is smooth; store in a tightly covered container in the refrigerator. This puree stays fresh for several weeks. **Yield: 1½ cups**

Per Tablespoon: **Calories:** 8.5 **Carbs:** 2.3g **Fiber:** 0.3g **Fat:** 0g **Sodium:** 0.3mg **Net Carbs:** 2g

Sweetened Condensed Milk

1 cup xylitol
1½ cups dry milk powder
4 tablespoons unsalted butter
½ cup plus 2 tablespoons boiling water

Place xylitol, milk powder, butter, and boiling water in blender; process for several minutes or until mixture is smooth. Store in refrigerator until ready to use. **Yield: 1¾ cups**

Per Tablespoon: **Calories:** 42 **Carbs:** 7.9g **Fiber:** 0g **Fat:** 1.7g **Sodium:** 20.3mg **Net Carbs:** 1.9g

Special Ingredients

This section is devoted to providing information and guidance concerning some of the ingredients used in the recipes in this book that may be unfamiliar to you. In compiling these recipes, I have focused on using primarily whole foods; however, I chose to use liqueurs to enhance the flavor of some of the recipes.

APPLESAUCE (UNSWEETENED): This is applesauce made entirely from apples and water. Apples are naturally sweet so an added sweetener is really unnecessary. This is an excellent substitute for some of the fat in recipes.

ARROWROOT POWDER: Arrowroot powder is a white, unrefined starch that is made from the root of a tropical American plant. It looks like cornstarch, is a natural thickening agent, and can be substituted for cornstarch on a one-for-one basis in pie fillings, sauces, and even ice creams. When substituting arrowroot for flour, use only half the amount of arrowroot. Arrowroot is inexpensive, and is available in health food stores.

CHOCOLATE BARS (SUGARLESS): Chocolate bars sweetened with xylitol, erythritol, and stevia are now available. I no longer recommend the use of chocolate sweetened with maltitol because of its high glycemic index and significant gastric side effects.

CHOCOLATE FOR BAKING (UNSWEETENED): This form of chocolate comes in bar form, and is made of pure chocolate. It works well in some recipes, and its major advantage is that xylitol can be added to increase the sweetness of the chocolate to a semi-sweet taste.

CHERRY FLAVORING: This is an essential ingredient to enhance the cherry flavor in some recipes. Normally, I prefer to use extracts, but in this case the cherry flavoring is preferred.

CHERRY LIQUEUR: This is a fruit liqueur produced from a distilling process using cherries. It is used to enhance the flavor of many cherry-based desserts.

COCONUT (UNSWEETENED, SHREDDED): Unsweetened and shredded or flaked coconut is available in health food stores. Fresh shredded coconut can be stored in a refrigerator for up to one week, or in a freezer for up to one year. Flaked coconut can be shredded in a food processor if the shredded product is not available.

CRÈME DE CACAO: This is a clear, chocolate-flavored liqueur produced from cocoa beans. It is a very popular liqueur and is often paired with crème de menthe in recipes.

continued on next page

continued from previous page

CRÈME DE MENTHE: This is a very popular peppermint-flavored liqueur available colorless or in a green color. It is often paired with crème de cacao in recipes.

CREAM OF TARTAR: This is a substance that can be added to egg whites while beating them to form meringue. Cream of tartar increases the meringue's volume, stabilizes it, and prevents it from becoming too dry.

EXTRACTS: These are available in a large variety of flavors, depending on the flavoring ingredient from which they are made. For example, vanilla extract is made from the vanilla bean. Use pure extracts, rather than flavorings, whenever possible. Exceptions are cherry flavoring and maple flavoring.

EXTRA VIRGIN OR VIRGIN OLIVE OIL: Olive oil's use over the centuries has proven it to be a stable, health-enhancing oil. Even though it is a poor source of essential fatty acids, it contains a high percentage of monounsaturated fatty acids that lower only the LDL or "bad cholesterol". If the olive oil is not labeled 'unrefined', the oil has undergone numerous refining processes, has been essentially stripped of any nutritional value, and has undergone molecular changes that can adversely affect our health. All virgin olive oils are unrefined, therefore, only virgin or extra virgin olive oils are recommended. Extra virgin olive oils are of the finest quality and must meet strict guidelines. When extra virgin olive oil is used in small quantities, the flavor of the basic recipe is not affected, and the taste of the olive oil is not detectable.

FRUIT SPREAD: The fruit spreads that are recommended for use in these recipes are sweetened only with fruit juices and contain no added sugar. Fruit spreads that are sweetened with xylitol or maltitol are also available.

GELATIN (UNFLAVORED): Gelatin is an animal by-product and is available in grocery stores. Kosher gelatin, which contains no animal products and may be preferred by vegetarians and vegans, is made from vegetable gum, tapioca dextrin, and acids. Powdered gelatin comes packaged four or more to a box. Each package contains 2 ¼ teaspoons of gelatin and will gel two cups of liquid. To soften gelatin, sprinkle it over a cold liquid and let stand for 2 to 3 minutes, then either warm the liquid, stirring until the gelatin is dissolved, or add a hot liquid to the gelatin mixture and stir until the gelatin is dissolved. Gelatin becomes firm when chilled in the refrigerator.

KAHLUA: Kahlua is a coffee-flavored liqueur.

LECITHIN GRANULES: Lecithin is a by-product of refined soybean oil. It is nutritious and helps to create a softer texture in breads, cakes, and cookies. The granules contain only about half the fat of butter. It is available in liquid and granular form; however, the granules are much easier to work with. Lecithin may be purchased at health food stores.

NON-FAT DRY MILK POWDER: This is whole milk that has had the fat and water removed, which means that the fat-soluble vitamins are also missing. However, this form of milk is excellent for use in recipes for whipped toppings and sweetened condensed milk so that xylitol can be used as the only sweetener.

PEANUT BUTTER: Be sure to select pure peanut butter made only from roasted peanuts with no sweetener added. Sometimes a small amount of salt is added to the peanut butter for flavor.

POWDERED XYLITOL: This is granulated xylitol that has been ground to a fine powder. It can be substituted for powdered sugar on a one-for-one basis. It is available commercially, or can be ground to a powder in a Vita-Mix or other machine of this type.

PRUNE PUREE: This is made by placing prunes and water in a blender and pureeing until the mixture is smooth. It is an excellent substitute for some of the fat in recipes.

SPELT FLOUR: Spelt is a type of "hard" wheat used since ancient times. Even though spelt contains gluten, many individuals with wheat allergies have found this grain to be more digestible and to cause fewer allergy problems than other gluten-containing grains. Spelt flour is available in health food stores.

TOFU: This is a soft, relatively tasteless food made from processed soybean curd. It may be purchased from health food stores and grocery stores.

TRIPLE SEC: This is an orange-flavored liqueur made from orange skins. It is less expensive and has less alcohol content than the other two orange-flavored liqueurs, Curacao and Grand Marnier, which may be substituted if desired.

UNSALTED BUTTER: Unsalted butter is much purer than salted

continued on next page

continued from previous page

butter and has a better flavor, in my opinion. Salt is usually added to butter to help preserve it and to mask any off-flavors and poor quality. I recommend that you use only U.S. Grade AA sweet cream unsalted butter.

WHOLE WHEAT PASTRY FLOUR: This is flour made from "soft" wheat that is more finely ground than regular whole-wheat flour. It may be used to replace all-purpose flour on a cup-for-cup basis.

YOGURT (LOW-FAT): Yogurt is made from milk that has had cultures added in order to make it curdle. It has the consistency of custard, and is a rich source of acidophilus and other beneficial bacteria. Plain yogurt is an excellent substitute for some of the fat in baked goods recipes. Most flavored yogurt sold commercially contains refined sugar, very little fruit, artificial colors and flavors, and many other ingredients to enhance its look and taste that add little or no nutritional value. If you want a more nutritious treat my recommendation is to purchase unflavored low-fat yogurt and add fruit and xylitol.

ZEST (GRATED LEMON OR ORANGE RIND): Grate only the colored part of the rind from these fruits, not the white portion under the rind as this has a bitter taste. Zest adds color and flavor to recipes. Always wash fruits thoroughly and dry them well prior to grating.

Choosing Cookware and Bakeware

I strongly recommend against using aluminum cookware and bakeware for several reasons. Aluminum pots and baking pans should not be used because most cooking utensils can easily scratch the inside surfaces which can cause some of the aluminum to be leached into the foods being cooked. The body then absorbs this leached aluminum when the food is eaten, and eventually it migrates into the cells of the brain and nervous system. It is suspected that an accumulation of excess aluminum in these organs is related to Alzheimer's disease, which is now one of the five leading causes of death in the United States. Also, when foods are cooked or stored in aluminum cookware, a substance that neutralizes the digestive juices can be produced, which may result in the development of acidosis and ulcers. However, aluminum bakeware can be used if the interior surfaces are coated with butter and then lined with parchment paper, which should also be buttered prior to adding the ingredients for baking.

Other cookware to be avoided includes all pots and pans with older non-stick coatings such as Teflon. These coatings, as a general rule, do not hold up well, and when scratched, they can flake off and react with the food being cooked in them. Ultimately, the chemicals in these coatings end up in the body. Newer bakeware with the harder non-stick coatings may be used as long as care is taken when removing food baked in them. This type of bakeware can be scratched, so use a plastic utensil to remove food from it instead of using a metal utensil or any other sharp object. If this bakeware becomes scratched, it may still be used if it is treated in the same manner as described above for aluminum bakeware.

Glass, stainless steel or cast iron are excellent choices for cookware and baking pans. I prefer to use Pyrex glass pie plates because the glass distributes the heat evenly and it is easy to determine visually when the crust is done. Stainless steel saucepans are excellent choices because they are very durable and easy to clean when the following suggestions are considered: (1) When cooking with gas, made sure that the flame touches only the bottom of the saucepan, and does not touch the sides of the pan; (2) Cool pots and pans prior to rinsing and soaking; (3) Don't allow an empty pan to sit on

continued on next page

continued from previous page

a hot burner, don't allow foods in the cookware to become so dry that they burn, and don't let liquids boil off completely; (4) Stainless steel is not a very good conductor of heat itself, so in choosing stainless steel cookware, select those brands that are made of a heavy gauge and have laminated copper or aluminum bottoms as this will help to evenly distribute the heat and prevent burning over high heat; (5) Use wood or one of the new plastic material utensils to avoid scarring or scratching the highly-polished interiors to make the cookware easier to keep clean.

Cast iron cookware is very versatile—it can be used in the oven or for range-top cooking—and if cared for properly, it will last practically forever. After it has been heated, it evenly distributes the heat and also retains it quite well. The secret to using cast iron cookware is to keep it seasoned to prevent rusting and to make it non-sticking. To season cast iron, spread salad oil on the inside, place in a 250° oven for several hours, and reapply the oil as it is absorbed. Remove the cookware from the oven and allow it to cool completely. Wipe off the excess oil with paper towels, and the cookware is now ready to use. Seasoned cast-iron cookware needs very little washing – just rinse under very hot water and wipe dry. Food comes out of cast-iron cookware very easily; however, as the seasoning wears off over time, food may begin to stick to it. To remove the stuck food, scrub the cookware with a plastic abrasive pad, and again follow the above directions to renew the seasoning. As an added protection against rusting, dry cast-iron cookware over medium-low heat for a few minutes after washing.

Index

About the Author

Karen Edwards has had a lifelong interest in cooking and became acquainted with natural methods of food preparation and the necessity for better nutrition through the La Leche League after the birth of her son. After developing several chronic health problems, she began to investigate non-traditional healing modalities. In order to gain a more thorough knowledge of natural healing and lifestyle modification, she enrolled in a doctoral program at Clayton College of Natural Health. Because of her intense interest in natural healing, she overcame the chronic health problems that had been affecting her. Upon completion and acceptance of her doctoral dissertation, "Reversing Periodontal Disease", she received her Ph.D. in Holistic Nutrition from Clayton College of Natural Health. She has served as a volunteer in a cooperative health food store, operated her own nutritional supplement store, and presented talks to various groups about healthy cooking methods and lifestyle changes. She currently resides with her husband in North Alabama.